Sonoran Desert Spring

#294

SENOR
DESRT
SPRNG
$15.95
+ tax

Sonoran Desert Spring

JOHN ALCOCK

Illustrated by Marilyn Hoff Stewart

THE UNIVERSITY OF ARIZONA PRESS

Tucson & London

The University of Arizona Press

Copyright © 1994 The Arizona Board of Regents

All rights reserved.

Licensed by the University of Chicago Press, Chicago, Illinois

© 1985 by The University of Chicago. All rights reserved.

∞ This book is printed on acid-free, archival-quality paper.

Manufactured in the United States of America

99 98 97 96 95 94   6 5 4 3 2 1

Library of Congress Cataloging-in-Publication Data

Alcock, John, 1942–

    Sonoran Desert spring / John Alcock.

      p.   cm.

    Originally published: Chicago : University of Chicago Press, © 1985.

    Includes bibliographical references (p.   ) and index.

    ISBN 0-8165-1399-6 (acid-free paper)

    1. Desert ecology – Sonoran Desert. 2. Spring – Sonoran Desert.

    3. Sonoran Desert. I. Title.

    [QH104.5.S58A4 1994]

    574.5'2652'0979173 – dc20   93-41190

                                                  CIP

British Cataloguing-in-Publication Data

A catalogue record for this book is available from the British Library.

For my friends

Contents

Preface to the Second Edition

Since *Sonoran Desert Spring* was first published, I have had the privilege of living in the Sonoran Desert of central Arizona for almost ten more years. Despite the press of ever more Arizonans, despite the growth of desert-destroying cities, despite the continuing ability of the livestock industry to run cows in every part of Arizona, despite everything, the Sonoran Desert is still one of the most beautiful and intriguing places on our planet. And I still derive great enjoyment from walking in the desert I call home and learning whatever I can about the plants and animals that live here too. I hope that my book can contribute to the desert enjoyment of other kindred spirits, persons who respect and love the desert for what it is and has to offer.

In this reprinting of the book, conducted under the auspices of the University of Arizona Press, I have made some small changes that bring the book up to date and correct a few errors that slipped into the earlier edition. But for the most part, I have left the text as it was when I first wrote it. The book was and is about the natural history of desert plants and animals that anyone with some patience, a little luck, and access to a patch of Sonoran Desert can see firsthand. There are still vast stretches where the great purple hairstreaks and teddy-bear chollas, the brittlebush and desert tortoise still roam. May my book help readers want to get to know them better and care about them always.

During the years prior to the initial publication of *Sonoran Desert Spring*, my research on insect behavior was funded intermittently by the National Science Foundation, for whose support I am grateful. I was also lucky in having some skillful coworkers, including David Post, John Schaefer, and Scott Snead. During these years, the chairs of the Department of Zoology at Arizona State University, Shelby Gerking, Ronald Alvarado, and Kathleen Church, consistently assisted me in my endeavors. I would also like to thank my colleagues, especially Ron Rutowski and Stuart Fisher, for their contributions to my work and to my enjoyment of the desert.

Susan E. Abrams of the University of Chicago Press encouraged me to write this book in the first place and provided me with a great deal of excellent editorial advice. I also received assistance from Kay Page and Ann Dinowitz. The current version of the book has been updated with help from Sue Alcock, Amy Chapman Smith, and Judith Wesley Allen. Marilyn Hoff Stewart has also provided seven new illustrations for this edition of the book, for which I thank her.

Sonoran Desert Spring

Illustration: Lupine

The Sonoran Desert

On a carefully manicured and recently watered embankment of the Superstition Freeway, a black-tailed jackrabbit sits in full view of rush-hour traffic. As cars thunder anonymously past, the rabbit breakfasts calmly on Bermuda grass.

A desert-dwelling jackrabbit is utterly different, a package of sinew, adrenalin, and terror that explodes from a hiding place among the creosote bushes and kicks off over the plain, sending gravel flying as it cuts from bush to bush. The soft, brown, delicate ears of the animal fold back as it darts under low-lying branches. In a few seconds it will be gone, leaving the observer with only flickering images of its escape.

The Superstition Freeway runs on through Mesa, Arizona, continuing east past housing developments and the cotton fields destined to become new housing developments, new mobile home parks, and new Circle Ks. The sun shines through the windshield.

Usery Pass Road intersects the freeway thirty minutes out of Phoenix. It runs north toward two mountains. Palo verde trees and ironwoods, cholla cacti and saguaros begin to appear in the spaces between the houses whose gardens feature Australian eucalyptus, Floridian tiff grass, and Mediterranean oleander. A roadrunner sprints across the highway and mounts the gravel berm on the far side; there it flashes open its wings and glides to safety among the desert shrubs — a modern-day vision of *Archeopteryx*.

Where the road reaches Usery Pass there are no houses yet, although the tops of hills near the border of the Tonto National Forest have been bulldozed flat, a vulgar preparation for the day when the developers will be able to build and sell there too.

Because it is early spring and there have been sufficient winter rains, the desert is green, and might, if one were generous, pass for a forest, although the tallest "trees" for miles are saguaro cacti. They rise in defiant punctuation from the desert scrub and rock.

On the west side of Usery Pass a multitude of dirt tracks break away from the main road. The desert here is seamed with these off-hand roads created by off-road vehicles. An empty white plastic jug lies discarded in a well-traveled sandy wash. The sun has bleached the once-brilliant lettering on the bottle. The track weaves unsteadily past a shallow but extensive gravel pit created by the Arizona Highway Department. Around the vast red scar of the pit, up a rise, is my habitual parking place at my research site in the Sonoran Desert.

The Sonoran Desert extends up from Mexico on either side of the Gulf of California into the United States, covering a region of more than one hundred thousand square miles, an area equal in size to the state of Arizona. Although this arid zone runs a short way into the southwestern corner of California, southern Arizona has the largest parcel of Sonoran Desert in this country. The desert is thought to have had its beginnings with the development of a semipermanent ridge of high pressure off the Californian and Mexican coasts some forty million years ago. This atmospheric feature dominates the weather of the region to this day by diverting storms that come off the north Pacific to the north of Arizona. When rains do reach southern California, they often fall largely over the cold coastal currents. Even showers that move onshore generally deposit their moisture on the hills near the ocean, leaving none for the area to the east. As a result, it is the rare storm that penetrates the Sonoran Desert. What little precipitation does fall comes as a rule from December to March as gentle rains from Pacific weather disturbances, or in late July and August as violent thunderstorms during the "monsoon" season, when low-pressure ridges pump moisture up from the Gulf of California. In an average year the Phoenix area receives about six inches of rain, but great annual variations make a mockery of average values. There are years when the desert waits parched and brown for rain that does not come.

Despite the aridity of the region and the intense heat of summer, when daily temperatures regularly reach or exceed 105 degrees, the land is far from barren. Although there are impressive sand dunes in northern Mexico, for the most part the desert is covered with vegetation in great and delightful variety. This is particularly true of the upland Sonoran areas, which are the subject of this book. The ancient age of the desert and its subtropical climate have combined to foster an extensive radiation of plant species beautifully adapted to cope with their demanding environment. Amid the desert vegetation live animals of an equally wonderful diversity whose ways of surviving also elicit admiration. This book describes some of the plants and animals found in the Usery Mountains of Arizona during the Sonoran spring, the time of year when the desert is most alive and accepting. My journal is an appreciation of desert life, the spring season in this marvelous arborescent wasteland, and the importance of places without people.

Usery Ridge

A number of hills rise dramatically from the sloping desert plain near Usery Pass. My parking area lies at the base of a ridge that invites inspection by persons willing to climb a steep trail. The roadside has its perennial smattering of debris donated by trash-dumpers and gunners who treat the desert with disdain. A mound of asphalt roofing shingles, a plastic cup emblazoned with the Circle K logo, three withered agave stumps, broken Coors bottles, and an arsenal of expended ammunition worthy of an army battalion rob the desert of its natural plainness and dignity.

A path that my feet have created dips down to a small dry wash, then runs directly to the foot of the ridge and up the ascending backbone of the hill. The amount of litter falls off sharply away from the dirt road. Most places in the desert that are more than a hundred paces from a roadway are relatively free of the detritus of human society, as civilized man fortunately has a limited capacity for bipedal locomotion.

The trail gains elevation quickly, and soon a vast Sonoran panorama greets the winded hiker. To the north, Four Peaks juts upward more than 7,600 feet, a somber gray presence in the spring and summer, often whitened with snow in the winter. To the northeast and northwest, the Salt and Verde rivers wind down toward Phoenix, which sprawls most of the year beneath its reddish inversion of toxic hydrocarbons.

Four dams within one hundred miles of Phoenix regulate the flow of the Salt River in order to trap as much water as possible for drinking, lawn watering, and cotton growing. Only when a vast excess of rainfall fills all four reservoirs does the Salt River

Project release sufficient water to send the Salt River charging through Phoenix. The Salt joins first the Gila River and then the Colorado River on its once-upon-a-time journey to the Gulf of California. (In most years the Colorado River's flow is also fully allocated to agricultural and municipal interests, so that the delta at the river's mouth remains dry and dusty.) From various vantage points on the ridge, Stewart Mountain Dam is visible to the north. So is the Granite Reef Diversion dam, which shunts the combined Salt and Verde River releases into the main irrigation channel leading to Phoenix. Below Granite Reef the riverbed lies empty and exposed, a broad sandy swath to the east.

The original and continuing mission of the Salt River Project has been to keep the four lake-reservoirs behind the upstream dams as full as possible so that no agricultural user need suffer water shortages. This goal requires management of the watershed of the Salt River, which is why the Tonto National Forest exists. The Tonto National Forest was named after the Tonto Apaches who still lived in the area in the late 1800s. This is all the recognition that the Apaches received for their efforts to cope with their hostile white neighbors. The whites used the Spanish word *tonto*, which means "stupid," to label the Indians whose land they exploited. When Roosevelt Dam, the first of the four, was built on the river at the turn of the century, the farmers in what is now metropolitan Phoenix formed the Salt River Valley Water Users' Association. In 1903 they lobbied in Washington to have the watershed of the Salt River made a national forest preserve, despite the contradictory wishes of sheep and cattle ranchers who wanted to graze their livestock on the land with little or no governmental interference. In 1905 the Tonto Forest was established over the objections of the ranchers, who since have had to secure grazing rights doled out with an eye to minimizing erosion and siltation. Three years later the forest was doubled in size to include a vast area of desert and grassland. Of the approximately three million acres that are currently part of the Tonto Forest, no more than 6 percent comprises commercially valuable timberlands, and more than half the land is not forest at all.

But placing the watershed of the lower Salt within the national

5

forest has meant that the area can be controlled to maximize run-off into the drainages that feed into the river and thence into the reservoirs. The U.S. Forest Service has removed chaparral growth from slopes in certain areas with herbicides or bulldozers, and it encourages cattle grazing in some locations to prevent the buildup of vegetation that would trap and use water that might better be employed by the inhabitants of Phoenix and surrounding Maricopa County.

The Usery Mountains have not been managed in this way; rainfall is so minimal here that additional runoff cannot be produced through alteration of the vegetation. In recent years even livestock grazing has been forbidden in the area so that the mountains, although hardly pristine, are at least reasonably undisturbed at the moment. As a happy by-product of the extension of the Tonto National Forest, Usery Ridge is federal, not private, property; those of us who wish to climb the ridge and learn about the lives of its plants and animals are completely free to do so. The real-estate developers must content themselves with despoiling the desert that lies several miles away on the border of federal lands. Otherwise they would surely have already begun to scrape, gouge, and shark their way through the flatlands that make up most of the vista visible from the ridge.

As it is, the great expanse of desert to the west and north is wonderfully devoid of human habitation. In the spring, when I come to the ridge most often, the vegetation on the plain endows the panorama with a healthy greenness — if winter rains have been generous.

Rocky outcrops and myriad washes, large and small, pattern the green desert with gray patches and pale brown lines. Most of the year the washes are dry ribbons of sandy gravel that curl their way toward the Salt River. But on rare occasions when there has been a sufficiently heavy rain to produce runoff, washes carry away the waters that gather in gullies on hill and mountain. Enough residual moisture remains in the gravelly soil to support denser-than-average populations of palo verde trees, ironwoods, and saguaro cacti on the borders of washes. But even here the vegetation rarely grows so thickly as to make things difficult for a walker.

6

The dispersed distribution of most plant species is still more pronounced across the desert plain and up the mountain slopes. Many Sonoran plants have extensive, shallow root systems for the collection of ephemeral water close to the surface. Competition for this water probably prevents the close packing of individuals; once it is established, a large saguaro's roots may remove water from a huge area, making it difficult for a younger plant to secure sufficient moisture to sustain itself within the province of the larger cactus.

In any case, the ample, fairly regular space that separates trees and shrubs from each other encourages the perception of each plant as an individual. During the spring months, the plants — jojoba and palo verde, small staghorn and giant saguaro cacti, grasses, minute flowers, even ferns and mosses in sheltered north-facing pockets — look alive and well.

Because the desert is all gravel and stony warts, the eroded hillsides form gigantic rock gardens. The reduced height and density of the foliage permits views from ridges and peaks that are rarely available in the almost impenetrable eastern forests, with their masses of seemingly undifferentiated vegetation. In contrast to the overwhelming lushness of such a forest, the desert in spring seems inviting, accessible, a mystery that might be solved.

The trail on Usery Ridge winds freely through the open vegetation, moving ever upward past ocotillo whose twelve-foot spiny whipstalks radiate out of the desert floor, through a patch of creosote bush that smells faintly of tar, past a prickly cholla cactus. The little palo verdes dot the ridge and slope, rarely rising more than ten feet from the ground.

The trail ends after less than a mile when it reaches the highest point for hundreds of yards around, a hilltop formed by the union of the main ridge with two others. Almost no one comes here, although occasionally I find a discarded cigarette butt or a collection of spent shotgun shells; nearby a freshly pocked and partially collapsed saguaro limb reveals how the visitor amused himself. Despite this depressing evidence of the presence of what I suppose I must claim as my fellow man, the climb to the peak invariably produces a pleasant exhilaration born of solitude and physical exertion. In the early spring the promise of new discoveries inspires each walk. The green bark of the palo verdes warmly accepts the morning sun. The haze of Phoenix is so far in the distance that by turning to face northwest, one can almost create the restoring illusion of wilderness.

February

Illustration: Robins and mistletoe in palo verde tree

Three Robins

S pring begins in February in the Sonoran Desert. The air warms by midday. The first grasses, having germinated after the rains of November and December, now appear as green tufts amid the unforgiving gravel. On the larger stones, black flies bask in the sun.

In a little hollow by the side of the trail, three robins feed on desert mistletoe growing on a limb of a palo verde. Mistletoe is a common parasite of many Sonoran trees and shrubs, but usually it attacks plants growing near washes. It produces an abundance of little greenish-white berries that gradually turn a muted red, not in the least ostentatious but attractive to human observer and avian consumer alike.

The robins create an Audubonesque tableau as they perch by the clump of mistletoe, reaching forward and delicately plucking a single berry at a time, their pale blue-gray backs luminescent in the filtered shade of the palo verde.

In five years of ridge walking this is the first time I have observed robins. Seeing them among Sonoran surroundings transforms them from backyard birds to be taken entirely for granted to rare and rewarding creatures. The advantage of the desert is that its spareness gives us new eyes and the time to focus on what we see. Here there are no jumbled woodlands filled with competing songs of dozens of species, no waves of migrant warblers in the giant treetops to lure a watcher from one bird to the next in a compulsive search for rarer species. On the ridge nothing is common, so each encounter with an animal, even the most familiar species, takes on special significance.

The aesthetic pleasure that comes from seeing robins on the

trail lies not only in their attractive plumage and surroundings, but also in the biological puzzles they pose. Mistletoes tend to be poisonous. But if this is true, how can robins eat the berries? And why should a plant produce conspicuous reddish fruits, albeit little ones, if they are toxic? Typically, conspicuous or advertised fruits evolve when a plant can benefit by attracting animals that will eat the fruits and disperse the seeds within. The "benefit" to an individual plant is measured by the number of its seeds that reach places where they can sprout and grow successfully into adults. Plants whose fruits attract relatively many good dispersers should have more impact on the evolution of their species, because they will on average leave more descendants than individuals that are ignored by animals that could effectively distribute their seeds. As it turns out, although mistletoe foliage may be noxious to some herbivores, the fruits are edible, consisting of a pulpy nutritious exterior that surrounds a few highly sticky seeds. Birds like robins and especially phainopeplas, the primary avian consumer of mistletoe berries, pass the fruits quickly through their digestive systems, removing the edible pulp and eliminating the seeds, which fall undigested wherever a bird chooses to deposit them.

Phainopeplas, the only North American representative of the silky flycatcher family, nest in the early spring in the mesquite bosques along Arizona streams and rivers in the Sonoran zone. The sleek black birds perch high in the trees so that when they defecate, any eliminated mistletoe seed has an excellent chance of striking a limb or branch on its way to the ground. Once a seed touches a limb, its glutinous covering helps it stick there, where it gives rise to rootlets that invade the host and begin to drain it of resources that the parasite uses for its own growth and reproduction. Not that mesquites are utterly defenseless: in some way the presence of a mistletoe seed may trigger the production of a resinous secretion that carries the seed up and away from the limb on which it rests. By placing the mistletoe seed on a pedestal, a mesquite can sometimes prevent the establishment of a seedling parasite.

Nonetheless mesquite forests are heavily infested with mistletoe, thanks in part to the unwitting assistance given the parasite by phainopeplas. In turn, the birds depend in considerable measure on the parasite, for they will not breed in places where mistletoe has failed to produce a good crop of berries (as happens, for example, after an unusual winter freeze). Although the adults feed their young primarily insects, they rely on berries for their own diet to such an extent that they cannot successfully reproduce if berries are in short supply.

This is then one of those cases in biology in which two unrelated species appear to cooperate to their mutual advantage; the mistletoe bribes the phainopepla with its fruit, and the bird disperses the seeds of the parasite. Examples of this sort seem to please most people, perhaps because we find the thought of cooperation among humans an appealing idea and its occurrence elsewhere a suggestion that harmony is a natural state of affairs, or at least a possible one.

What is often overlooked, however, is that the union of forces among cooperators generally has as its goal the destructive exploitation of a third party. Phainopepla and mistletoe may be good for one another, but the riparian honey mesquite and palo verde suffer a great deal as a result of their harmonious interaction. A severely infested tree may even die under its burden of parasitic mistletoe.

A closer look might also reveal that cooperators would exploit one another given the chance but do not because of the counterdefenses each has evolved against the other. Phainopeplas do not digest mistletoe seeds but defecate them whole and uninjured. Why? A person with a benign view of nature might claim that by helping the mistletoe, the bird insures future supplies of berries for other members of its species. But few evolutionary biologists would consider this a plausible hypothesis. Imagine that in a population composed of helpful "Johnny-mistletoe" types, there appeared by mutation a phainopepla capable of digesting mistletoe seeds. The fate of the distinctive hereditary basis for seed digestion would depend *only* on the immediate reproductive success of bearers of the new gene — not on the contribution the trait made to the preservation of the species as a whole. If "selfish" digesters consistently left more descendants than the other birds,

13

after many generations phainopepla populations would contain only seed digesters; the Johnny-mistletoe types would have been eliminated because of their lower rate of reproduction.

Any hypothesis, therefore, suggesting that a characteristic has evolved for the reproductive benefit of someone other than the individual that exhibits the trait is logically suspect. Phainopeplas do not digest mistletoe seeds, probably because there is some immediate reproductive advantage to themselves in eliminating seeds whole. I suspect that mistletoe seeds are either toxic or so hard-coated that any nutritive benefit derived from dissolving the coat would be outweighed by the metabolic costs of extracting the nutrients. This hypothesis remains to be tested, but at least we can see, thanks to evolutionary logic, that a true puzzle exists in the failure of robins and phainopeplas to digest fully the seeds of fruits they consume. Problems are often as captivating as answers in biology; a walk on Usery Ridge amid Sonoran plants and animals provides a host of entertaining questions as well as the time to digest them.

White-throated Swifts

swarm of midges hovers above the palo verde growing on
the peaktop at the end of the trail. The minute flies dart
and weave among the branch tips to a tune of their own making.
On many early spring days a brisk, even chilly wind slices over
the peak on its way through Usery Pass. But today the air is still.
The mountains on the western horizon forty miles away look
clean and smooth, their canyons, gullies, and rocky outcrops
erased by the distance. The trilling call of a rock wren rises to
the ridge.

An explosive bull-roaring snap cuts the air just behind me and
ends the reverie of the moment. Heart pounding, I look in time
to identify a rocketing white-throated swift. If ever an animal de-
served the name "swift," this bird does. By the time I regain my
composure it has hurtled hundreds of feet down the ridge, traveling like a white-throated missile with wings.

Biologists place white-throated swifts in a genus with the su-
perbly appropriate name *Aeronautes*. They are indeed true aero-
nauts for whom flight seems an end in itself. In the Usery area
they appear regularly in spring, rifling through the sky in self-
absorbed pursuit of small insects that swarm in mating clusters
above the hilltops.

In keeping with their aeronautical appellation, white-throated
swifts are one of the few birds to copulate in the air. A male
catches a female high in the sky; the two swifts together then spin
slowly part way to earth like a giant paired maple seed.

Swifts as a group are unusual not only for their ability to copulate on the wing but also because of their nesting behavior. Some
species nest exclusively in recessed areas behind waterfalls; others

construct their nests entirely with their own saliva. An Asian swift creates a tiny cup nest just large enough for one egg, which it glues into the nest with salivary secretions. In their own way, white-throated swifts have evolved a remarkable ability related to nesting. Once in southern Utah I watched the birds come shooting down a canyon to sweep straight up into a crack in the overhanging rock wall. In this all-but-inaccessible crevice within the dark interior rock face, the swifts had a safe place to glue their nests. Their capacity to fly at top speed into a six-inch-wide opening in a rock wall is testimony to their command of the air.

The swift displays its speed and aerial agility most spectacularly in what look like games of follow-the-leader. Occasionally during the breeding season, threesomes of swifts rush past the peak, turning and twisting in an exquisite ballet. The two followers mimic with grace and perfection every move of the leading swift. But what is the point of these aerial chases? The trios probably consist of a female pursued by her mate (the second bird) and a would-be sexual interloper (the third bird, also a male). In a number of other species of birds a male will leave his partner for a time after her eggs have been fertilized. He invests this time in pursuit of other paired females in an attempt to gain some extracurricular copulations. In some way, males can identify gravid females whose eggs they might still fertilize, and they try to inseminate these individuals. The paired partner of a gravid female responds to this threat by guarding her. This he accomplishes by flying with his mate wherever she goes during the few days when her eggs can be fertilized. Through the close surveillance of his partner, a male decreases the probability that she will receive sperm from a rival, increases the chance that he will actually fertilize his partner, and helps guarantee that the offspring he will later protect and feed will be his own, not those of an interloping male.

An interpretation of this sort recognizes that evolution occurs not to preserve species but simply because different individuals in the past had varying abilities to propagate their distinctive genetic material. Again, we can imagine a population in the past with two kinds of male swifts. One type protected his mate when her eggs

16

could be fertilized and later attempted to steal egg fertilizations from the partners of other males; the second kind of male only attempted to inseminate the female whose offspring he would later help to rear. The "hypersexed" males should tend to fertilize more eggs and therefore pass on more of their distinctive genes than the genetically different "faithful" males. If this were true, eventually the genetic basis for "faithful" behavior in males would be eliminated from the population of swifts, even though the frantic competition among hypersexed males would not increase the fecundity of females of their population one iota. In fact, constant harassment by such males doubtless consumes time and energy that females could devote to other more productive activities.

Just as we can expect phainopeplas to employ a feeding strategy that maximizes individual gain, so too male swifts should behave in ways that promote their reproductive success *as individuals*, even if this reduces the long-term success of the species as a whole. The view that descendant-leaving competition is at the heart of evolution provides a biological philosophy that can inform and guide an analysis of all living things, from a sedentary clump of red-berried mistletoe anchored on a mesquite limb to a free-flying swift — noisy, exuberant, dismissive of men, living its life in the fast lane.

Clouds

Dewdrops reveal the otherwise hidden patches of spider silk that lie flat upon the spring grasses. A small gray fly alights on a sparkling silken sheet and then, as if aware of its mistake, attempts to leave. But although it is able to walk on the silk, it cannot fly free. A black spider emerges from a silken funnel and moves first hesitantly and then confidently toward the fly, grasping it in a black-legged embrace.

Row upon row of puffy clouds push north. Avenues of sunshine flow up and down the east-west ridges and then sail out over the plain below, illuminating thin cross sections of desert vegetation.

Two red-tailed hawks take advantage of the wind to circle, swoop, and dive in aerial ballets that establish a bond between male and female. Far below the exuberant hawks a desert tortoise in search of sunshine stands stolidly on desert pavement. Muddy patches besmear its sturdy back. A thin paste of green outlines the tortoise's beaklike mouth, traces of his recent meal. With unblinking eye the reptile stares into the desert.

March

Illustration: Tarantula hawk on flowers of foothills palo verde

The Great Purple Hairstreak

An afternoon west wind sweeps the rocky slope of the ridge and a red-tailed hawk confidently coasts on the updraft. From time to time it casually tilts one wing or alters the angle of its tail feathers as it spirals slowly upward. Having achieved sufficient altitude, the hawk banks to drift out over the great basin to the west. For a moment its red tail gleams in the sunlight.

A great purple hairstreak inspects its more limited domain from a perch atop palo verde #5 (one of eighteen of the more prominent palo verdes growing along the ascending ridge to which I have assigned a number in the past, the better to record their occupants). Although the hairstreak lacks the size and drama of a swallowtail or monarch butterfly, it artfully compensates with shining black wings marked by small dots of red and white and a large patch of iridescent blue, in addition to a shockingly orange abdomen, black eyes, and white head. (There is not a trace of purple anywhere on its body, creating the aggravating mystery of how it could ever have been labeled the great *purple* hairstreak.)

As the butterfly rests on its twig perch, it holds its wings tightly together and deliberately rubs its hindwings up and down, keeping in motion a bluish-lobed projection and two hairlike extensions of each lower hindwing. The wind swirls through the tree, obscuring the distant sounds of occasional cars racing through what might as well be another universe.

Hindwing rubbing by perched hairstreaks is such a distinctive idiosyncrasy of the group that lepidopterists have long wondered how it might improve the descendant-leaving success of individual butterflies. The "false head" hypothesis argues that habitual movement of the hindwings distracts predators from the hairstreak's actual head. The lobes and hairs on the hindwings of many species of hairstreaks look rather like the head of a butterfly with antennae; a predator drawn by the appearance and movements of the wings might attack this region first. The attack might well remove the false head, but the butterfly would be much more likely to live and reproduce without a portion of its hindwings than without a portion of its head. I have occasionally seen great purple hairstreaks with V-shaped notches removed from their hindwings, clipping off the tail region but not destroying the butterfly's ability to fly. Symmetrical wing damage of this sort has been linked to attack by birds whose beaks snap over the folded wings, clipping out a V-shaped patch of expendable hindwing while the rest of the butterfly departs essentially unharmed.

The false-head hypothesis has been rigorously tested in an ingenious manner. Robert Robbins predicted that he would find a correlation between the elaborateness of the tail region and the frequency of beak damage in this area. There are many species of hairstreaks, some with conspicuous hindwings, others with less dramatic "false heads." Presumably the more striking the tails, the more likely they are to attract an attacking bird and the more often they should be removed during an attack, *if* the false head functions to deflect predatory attack. In a sample of South American species, the hairstreaks with more elaborate tail regions were, as predicted, more apt to be beak-marked than butterflies with less complex false heads.

Many other questions remain about the behavior of great purple hairstreaks. Experience has taught me that if I see a perched hairstreak, it will be a male, and furthermore, that there will almost always be only one male to a tree. Moreover, the hairstreaks regularly occupy only a handful of the palo verdes on the ridge. There is always an excellent chance that palo verde #17 will have a male resident when I canvass the trees along the trail, but the odds are poor that palo verde #14 will gleam with a hairstreak on a spring afternoon.

Do individual males hold the same tree for the duration of an afternoon? Do they return to that tree on subsequent days? These questions require that one be able to recognize individual butterflies, and this requires that they be marked in distinctive ways. To mark a great purple hairstreak, one can place a small blob of enamel paint on a twig and attempt to dab the wings of the butterfly while it perches in a tree. I use the word "attempt" advisedly because hairstreaks, although not nearly as skittish as many other butterflies, are neither blind nor altogether lacking in caution; more often than not, the insect will dart up from his perch just as I am about to apply the paint to his wings. Even more aggravating are those occasions when I have succeeded in touching the wings of the butterfly only to learn when the male returns from his startled flight around the tree that no paint has adhered to his wings. The enamel paint has a way of drying on the twig before I can make contact with my "victim." Therefore, I sometimes employ the less frustrating and more direct method of capturing the hairstreak with a sweep of my insect net. Once in the net, the butterfly can be restrained, marked through the mesh of the net with paint or Liquid Paper, and released. This method has the advantage of rarely failing to produce a marked male, but it has the unprofitable result of terrorizing the hairstreaks. They become completely unhinged once confined in the folds of an insect net. From the moment of capture until it is restrained, a hairstreak beats its wings furiously in a futile effort to fly through the mesh. This can damage the insect's wings, and upon release, some males depart looking rather the worse for wear. I wonder whether this experience might not weaken some individuals and cause others to abandon their trees sooner than they would have otherwise.

Despite the drawbacks associated with both methods of marking great purple hairstreaks, it is a practice with a great many rewards, because some marked individuals do return to the palo verde trees they had been using. One's perception of an insect (or any other animal for that matter) is wonderfully transformed when one can recognize it as a particular individual. Over the years some marked males have resided in certain trees for as long as three weeks, and many others have been around for a week or so. It is easy to come to view these animals as old friends and to be disappointed when, inevitably, "yellow two dots right hindwing" or "pink left forewing" is gone from his customary perch, and an unmarked individual occupies its place.

The knowledge that some males return to favored perch sites raises still more questions. Why is it that only males are found in palo verdes, and what are they waiting for? Although human males will have no trouble providing an intuitive answer to the second part of the question, the scientific way to piece together the puzzle of the lives of hairstreaks is primitively simple in its conception. One sits and watches perched males. This is not always the most stimulating or comfortable of occupations, for much of the time great purple hairstreaks do little or nothing except perch, and the gravel and rocks of the hilltops do not make restful sitting places. Nevertheless, from time to time the hairstreak under inspection will enliven the watching by flying out from its perch to spring around the tree, black-and-blue wings snapping in the afternoon breeze, before it returns (usually) to alight close to its original perch.

The real excitement comes on those relatively rare occasions when another hairstreak wings into view. Almost without exception this creature proves to be another male, and the response of the resident hairstreak is swift and dramatic. He leaves his perch to fly out directly at the newcomer, whom he engages in a race once or twice or thrice around the palo verde. This is often the end of the interaction, for one male usually departs while the other lands in the tree. If the original resident has been marked, the odds are nearly perfect that it will be the familiar paint-dotted individual who returns to perch on the palo verde.

Although most male-male encounters consist only of these abbreviated chases, sometimes the race about the palo verde evolves into a "spiral flight." In these interactions, one male leads the other on a nearly vertical flight fifty, one hundred, two or three hundred feet into the air. Typically the two males are so close together that as they climb, they circle one another. On a still day one can sometimes hear the whispering clash of butterfly wings.

After reaching the apex of their spiral, the two males come diving down toward the earth like insect kamikaze pilots. But rather than commit suicide on his mission, one male will pull out of his

24

dive to head for the palo verde tree in a pell-mell rush while the other individual usually heads along the ridge, leaving his rival in control of the tree. As with less dramatic chases, residents usually "win" these contests; they typically are the ones to return to their palo verdes after a spiral flight. But sometimes an intruder does not retreat. Instead, he engages the resident in one spiral flight after another until eventually the old resident gives up and the victorious newcomer claims the tree.

Thus, although spiral flights may not seem to be particularly direct ways of fighting, they are the hairstreak's way of determining ownership of a perch territory. A male simply does not tolerate another's presence in his palo verde. I interpret the spiral flight as an effective way for males to demonstrate their speed, aerial agility, and endurance to one another, and I suspect that a male that can not keep up with his opponent abandons the palo verde rather than continue in fruitless attempts to fly higher or faster than his aerial duelist.

Now why might male hairstreaks use these apparently gentlemanly dogfights to determine who gets to perch in a given palo verde? I can only guess at the answer to this question, but there are other "hilltopping" male insects that behave in much the same way. In these species males pursue passing females, capturing them in flight and then descending with them to the earth where they copulate. If great purple hairstreaks do the same thing (and I have only partial evidence that they do), then males may be defending good places from which to spot possible mates and may use racing challenges to reach an (unconscious) decision about whether it would pay to remain at a particular location. I assume it would not be advantageous for a given hairstreak to remain if it had to contend with a faster or more agile opponent that would surely win the race to reach a passing female. Such persistent losers would leave fewer descendants than ones that went in search of alternative sites where females might be encountered without a faster, stronger competitor nearby.

My speculations on these matters are hampered by the stubborn refusal of female hairstreaks to present themselves to the waiting males I am watching. Despite many hours of observation,

I have yet to see a female pass by a male's perch, attract the male, and mate. Thus whenever I walk the ridge in the months when male hairstreaks occupy the palo verdes, I have a special reason to keep an eye on the trees. Someday I hope to see a male race successfully after a flying female. This sight would add materially to my understanding of why male hairstreaks spend the afternoon hours waiting and fighting, only to wait some more. For the time being I content myself with a partial knowledge of their lives. There is probably no other kind of knowledge in biology.

Tarantula Hawks

The first of the male tarantula hawks to claim a territory this season is back on his perch today on a branch tip in palo verde #17. He has two bright blue paint dots on his dull black thorax, a memento of our first encounter three days ago. Although this year these impressively big black wasps emerged and arrived on the ridge almost a month earlier than in previous years, their territorial preferences have remained consistent. As usual, palo verdes #10 and #17 were the first to be occupied; today there is a third male on the lookout in palo verde #8 lower on the ridge.

The male in the peaktop palo verde is a relatively large individual about two inches long, with rich reddish brown wings that gleam in the sunshine today. Within a few weeks, if he should survive that long, they will be dulled and frayed from hours of flight time. I will probably see him at his post for about a week before he is gone and a new resident is in his place.

Another tarantula hawk circles an ocotillo on its way up to the peak. A perched ash-throated flycatcher cocks its head and inspects the cruising wasp with a baleful eye but makes no attempt to capture the prey. A wasp in the hand smells foully acrid, and I suspect that they are not appetizing food for insect-hunting birds.

The flying wasp passes the flycatcher and heads steadily toward the crown of palo verde #17. The much larger resident catapults from his perch. The two insects race about the tree, exchanging the lead, and then ascend, first at a modest angle and then almost vertically, spiraling about each other for a climb of eighty feet. Out of the sky they plummet, the large wasp making for the palo verde, the other male descending down along the side ridge. The resident circles his tree several times and then clumsily lands on a perch twig, almost falling before pulling himself upright with long, black, spiny legs to assume a watchful stance once again.

A ladybird beetle ambles mechanically along a maze of palo verde twigs, unaware of the drama played out in the clear blue sky above it.

Female tarantula hawks rarely appear on the ridge. On average they are substantially larger than the males. An adult female may be three to four inches long, excluding the gleaming black, half-inch stinger that she normally carries within her body. She extrudes it when she wishes to subdue a spider or make an assailant wish very much that it had grasped something else. The sting is said to be intensely painful. I cannot describe the sensation first-hand; some years ago I was so impressed by the dimensions of the stinger of a female wasp in my insect net that I resolved to take every precaution to avoid contact with it. The enormously large stinger darting through the mesh of an insect net is an intimidating sight.

I am fortunate that my studies concern male behavior because male wasps lack stingers (which are evolved modifications of the female's egg-laying organ or ovipositor). Before I began watching tarantula hawks on the ridge, essentially nothing was known about male behavior in these insects. Traditionally those few scientists around the world who study wasp behavior have focused on the females of the species, which are certainly worth learning about. In highly social insects such as paper wasps, honeybees, and ants, there are two kinds of females: queens and workers. Egg-laying is the all-consuming occupation of the one or several queens that dominate a colony of social insects. For example, a queen honeybee in one spring day may deposit fifteen hundred eggs, which together weigh about as much as she does. To achieve feats of this sort, queens require constant feeding and care, and this is provided by their workers, which in many species are the queen's daughters. A honeybee worker builds brood comb, distributes food to her mother and the larval grubs in their nest cells, forages for pollen and nectar, cools or heats the hive according to its need, and attacks and repels hive robbers. The capacity of the tens of thousands of bees in a colony to coordinate their various activities is a wonderful thing. The great complexity of communication in social insects and the evolution of sterility in the worker force are major puzzles for biologists, and one way to contribute to the solution of the puzzle is to conduct thorough studies of the behavior of females in the appropriate species.

Females of solitary bees and wasps do not live with sterile worker offspring, but they too have attracted considerable attention because of their diverse and remarkable parental behaviors. It is they who dig the nest burrows and provision the cells with food for their offspring. Species vary greatly in the prey they select, the manner in which they carry it to the nest, the schedule on which offspring within the nest are provided with food, and so on.

Female tarantula hawks — and there are a number of species even in Arizona alone — are solitary wasps that are justly famous for their ability to tackle large spiders, notably tarantulas, which they are able to paralyze despite the spider's formidable jaws. Once a female has inserted her stupendous stinger into the thorax of her prey, she either uses the spider's own burrow as a brood chamber or drags her paralyzed but still-living victim to a suitable crevice. In either case, the wasp lays an egg on the entombed spider, closes off the burrow, and leaves her prey in the gentle company of her offspring, which will eventually hatch out into a predatory grub that devours the spider. Paralysis keeps the prey fresh for the gluttonous grub. After polishing off the spider, the grub eventually undergoes metamorphosis to a pupal stage; finally, the next spring, it changes into an adult, scrabbles out of the nest burrow, and flies off to begin its reproductive phase.

Compared with the intrigue and adventure of female wasps, the generally less conspicuous activities of the males have attracted less research attention. But in reality male tarantula hawks lead lives that are in some ways as exciting as those of their females. Males of "my" species, *Hemipepsis ustulata*, behave in a manner that is remarkably similar to the behavior of the great purple hairstreak. Like hairstreaks, male tarantula hawks do not tolerate other males in their perch trees, so that a resident in a palo verde

29

attempts to prevent visitors from landing in his tree. The two species defend many of the same palo verdes, the wasps generally in the morning, the hairstreaks taking over in the afternoon. The methods used by tarantula hawks to deal with intruders are essentially identical to the tactics of the hairstreak. Incoming males are "greeted" in flight, chased about the palo verde, and if they do not leave promptly, challenged to a spiral flight. Usually the spiraling wasps reach heights of fifty to one hundred fifty feet, but on occasion I have watched a pair through binoculars only to have them travel upward out of sight. Like the hairstreaks, tarantula hawks terminate the ascent phase of their flight with an abrupt dive earthward at tremendous speed. One or both wasps return to the palo verde from which the resident flew. Unlike the hairstreaks, male tarantula hawks commonly engage in a long series of spiral flights, one following the other at the rate of about three to four per minute for periods of an hour or even longer in extreme cases. Typically the original resident eventually returns to perch in his palo verde tree while the newcomer flies off into the distance, but sometimes, especially after a long series of spiral flights, possession of the perch site passes from one male to the other.

Why is it that tarantula hawk and great purple hairstreak males have evolved such similar behavior? We might rephrase this question to ask what similar pressures make waiting at and defending prominent landmarks the most profitable reproductive option for males of these two unrelated insect species. The assumption must be that those males that have reproduced most often in the past have shaped the history of their species; the current representatives of the wasps and butterflies are descended from reproductively successful ancestors, not from reproductive failures. The living members of each species should therefore possess the hereditary basis for the development of behavioral tactics that best overcome the obstacles to locating mates.

When we compare the tarantula hawk and the hairstreak, we discover that both are relatively uncommon animals that are widely dispersed. When I walk through the desert scrub below the ridge or along the riparian border of the Salt River, I almost never come across a single tarantula hawk or great purple hairstreak. Not only is the overall population of these insects small, but there is nothing in their lives that would tend to encourage females (and hence mate-searching males) to concentrate in certain parts of the desert. Females of both species feed on nectar from any of a great variety of common flowering plants. Therefore, a male that defended a blooming creosote bush or a patch of annuals would have little chance of securing a mate in return for his efforts. Moreover, the spiders that the wasps hunt are distributed more or less evenly rather than in dense and defendable patches; the hairstreaks lay their eggs on desert mistletoe, the common parasitic plant whose berries feed the phainopeplas and migrating robins. A male butterfly guarding a clump of mistletoe or an eager wasp holding sway over a section of rocky slope would surely have a long wait before his investment of time and energy was repaid by mating with a female attracted to the resources under his control.

Given the drawbacks associated with a "resource-defense" strategy, perhaps males can mate more often by locating lookout points from which they can scan most effectively for females traveling between two feeding or oviposition sites. Originally a male with a tendency to perch and wait in good lookouts might have left more descendants than those that searched elsewhere. Subsequently there might have been competition among males for superior elevated perches and selection in favor of females that came specifically to these places, for they could mate quickly and get on with the important tasks of producing and laying eggs.

Admittedly scenarios of this sort contain a large element of speculation, but the correlation between highly dispersed, relatively uncommon females and the use of hilltop landmarks by waiting males applies to more species than just the tarantula hawks and hairstreaks. Consistent relationships of this sort provide encouragement for those of us who would like to believe that the behavior of animals makes evolutionary sense. If it does nothing else, the search for patterns in the ecology and lives of the animals on the ridge gives meaning to my excursions to the desert, and I am grateful for the justification.

The tarantula hawk in palo verde #17 is doubtless unaware that the history of his species is reflected in the particular genes that reside within his body and that have helped shape the design of his nervous system. His small but elaborate waspish brain provides him with the capacity to fly to the highest palo verde tree, perch competently in its outer twigs, silhouetted against the sky above the mountains, and wait with every indication of expectancy.

There is little reason for optimism on his part. In hundreds of hours of observation I have seen only a handful of matings, a puzzle in itself because at times there may be as many as eighteen resident males and at least an equal number of cruising intruders along the ridge. Why there is not an equivalent number of females is a question for which I have no answer. But every once in a long while a huge female sails past a palo verde, triggering hot pursuit by the resident male. When he captures the female, the pair glide to earth and copulate for a minute or so after only the most rudimentary courtship. After male and female separate, she resumes her ponderous flight and he returns to wait in his palo verde for another rare opportunity to mate.

Spring after spring, in late March or early April, a new generation of males begins to emerge from brood chambers. The wasps make their way to the ridge where they claim the same palo verdes as their ancestors. In defense of their perches they spiral into the Arizona sky in the same combative way as always and wait with inexhaustible patience for females to arrive. They are a symbol of the Sonoran spring, serenely independent, unknown to most humans below, repeating a cycle of life that bears the imprint of the past.

Diamondbacks

The mood on the ridge changes over the course of the day from one of energy in the early morning to midday passivity. Now in the late afternoon, sullenness hangs in the air. The sun descends in the west. The birds have ceased to sing. Deep shadows fill the ravines and flood the washes. The desert poppies have pulled their petals into closed packages, extinguishing their radiant orangeness.

The last hairstreak has abandoned his palo verde perch for the day, and I follow his lead taking a new route down the ridge, using the larger rocks on the hillside as steps in a freelance stairway. The handle of my insect net serves as a staff to steady my descent. About halfway down I set the butt of my staff on a diamondback rattlesnake basking in a remnant patch of sunshine at the base of my stepping stone. Our encounter surprises us both.

The pale flesh-colored rattles on the tail of the snake begin to move and blur before my eyes. A malevolent buzz sends electric messages to the base of my brain. My feet are rooted to the ground. The snake's beautiful diamondbacked body uncoils and slides into the shelter of a jojoba bush. A small bee foraging late hangs from a pale jojoba flower. I wait for a moment, heart pounding, before looping carefully about the bush to continue my downward journey.

Diamondbacks are neither common nor conspicuous during the day on Usery Ridge. I probably see a rattler once in about a hundred hours of walking, and I doubt that persons not specifically searching for them would encounter diamondbacks more often. Those snakes that I do see usually rattle long before they are about to be stepped on. Perhaps this silent individual was cold and sluggish, only becoming aroused when my net handle touched him. But why do rattlesnakes rattle?

We can be confident that rattling has not evolved purely to protect humans and other animals that may encounter diamondbacks. Instead, in the past at least, there must have been a survival advantage for snakes prone to rattle in some situations. Rattling probably evolved in the context of encounters between snakes and their potential enemies, such as coyotes and roadrunners.

At one time in the distant past, tail-vibrating may have been the reptilian analogue of hind-wing rubbing by hairstreaks. Attracted by the movement of the snake's tail, predators might have tended to attack the expendable tail tip rather then the vital head of the diamondback, enabling the reptile to survive and use its fangs to poison and repel the enemy. Any variant snake capable of producing a rattling sound would have heightened the attention-getting nature of the distraction display. Once this stage had been reached, a diamondback could communicate at a considerable distance with potential predators or other large mammals that could damage it by stepping on it. The buzzing sound announces that the snake is alert and prepared to use its venom against anything that approaches. Under many circumstances it would be advantageous for both actors in the drama to withdraw, rather than interact and run the risk of death or injury; thus the diamondback, as well as the other animal, could benefit from the heart-stopping warning of the snake.

The arrival of humans in the Southwest, however, has created a novel selection pressure on rattlesnakes. The snakes' warning may now tend to decrease, rather than increase, their opportunities for survival and future reproduction. Most of my fellow Arizonans go out of their way to dispatch *any* snake that comes their way, but rattlers arouse a special hatred, distilled from equal parts of fear and self-righteousness, and the snakes are attacked with a correspondingly ferocious self-satisfaction. It is surprising that any noisy rattlers still exist because once detected, the chance that a rattler will escape from a human is almost nil.

Some nonpoisonous snakes that rely on speed rather than camouflage and ambush to capture their prey can slither off so quickly that their would-be tormentors are left gaping. But a coiled rattle-snake, big-bodied and slow, is close to defenseless against a gun, stick, or stone. The only satisfying aspect of the unequal contests between man and snake is that once in a while a killer handles his victim prematurely. Rattlers thought to be moribund have been known to revive long enough to sink their fangs into persons who were inspecting their trophies. Most rattlesnake bites occur through human stupidity or carelessness of this sort, but even when these self-induced injuries are figured into the equation, the risk that someone in the United States will be poisoned by any venomous animal is twenty times less than the risk of being struck by lightning and three hundred times less than the risk of being murdered by another human being. (Here the "risk" is figured in terms of average number of days of life expectancy lost because of encounters with poisonous animals, lightning, or murderers.) In recent memory, almost no one has died of a rattle-snake bite.

Even if this information were widely broadcast, I doubt it would greatly reduce the jubilant mayhem perpetrated on snakes. So elemental is the human fear of reptiles that the impulse to destroy rattlers would probably persist in the face of the most rational arguments. I must confess that when I walk through the desert, especially in areas with reasonably dense, low-lying cover, the image of a venomous snake lurking in ambush flickers with annoying frequency through my thoughts. There is always the suspicion that the next step will be not on *terra firma* but on *reptilia infirma*, creating a sensation that would be familiar to a soldier on a mission through a minefield. More than once the nearby rustle of a whiptail lizard in the undergrowth or the startled stridulation of a cicada has sent my heart rate skyrocketing. But only a real snake can reduce me to abject terror. Once when I came up the ridge trail on the double, I nearly ran into a big rattler with its triangular head reared at knee level, tail electrifying the air with its sibilant rattling. I have never come so quickly to a complete halt. After freezing, I eventually backed off to safety, each step sending the snake into a new spasm of venomous buzzing.

An encounter with a diamondback is wonderfully stimulating

to the imagination. For the rest of such a day, if not on subsequent days as well, brown fallen limbs of palo verdes, coils of dried mosses lying along the edge of a rock, even elongate stones are transformed one and all into hidden snakes. The pseudometamorphosis lasts just a fraction of a second, but long enough to stimulate the adrenals. I find now that even when I go to places where there are no poisonous snakes, my Sonoran habits, established in the persistent tenseness of the desert, continue to affect my behavior. I catch myself checking likely places for snakes, coming up short for a millisecond or two when a snake-mimicking limb on the forest floor activates my visual cortex before the "false alarm" cells in my brain can regain control. So although they are rare and hardly a statistically significant risk to life or limb, rattlers do have a continuing emotional grip on those of us who live with them. They keep wilderness in the spirit of the desert, and I hope they will survive to perform this service for generations to come.

April

Illustration: Hedgehog cactus

Desert Annuals

A large gopher snake half slithers, half falls from the palo verde in which it has been climbing. It glides through a lush stand of low desert growth of poppies, lupines, and bursage. The whispery sounds of its body crossing the gravelly soil and the movement of a trembling plant here and there reveal the departing snake's path.

Beside a wash at the base of the ridge a resonant hum fills the air. A plump swarm of honeybees hangs from a branch clustered in the center of a small thorny acacia. Now that it is early April, large and healthy colonies of honeybees have begun to divide; the old queen becomes a pioneer, leaving her previous homesite to a daughter and a retinue of half her workers. With the other half of her helpers she flies to a staging area such as a protective acacia or mesquite. There she and most of her court cluster together in a swarm for several days, while scout bees from the group fan out to find a new shelter for the colony.

In the coolness of early morning only a few scout bees drift out to search for a new homesite. Instead, workers whirr their wings to generate heat for their companions and for their queen, hidden beneath a mound of bee bodies. As the day progresses and temperatures rise, the swarm will hum with activity as hundreds of bees travel out and back with information on potential living places.

On the hillside, hairy-leaved fiddlenecks have begun to turn from green to brown. A month ago patches of the weedy plant luxuriated in shady places beneath palo verdes and creosote bushes. The long stalks curled over elegantly at the top, bearing a fresh abundance of little yellow flowers. Now the arms of some plants, once vertical, have grown overlong and lie twisted in all directions, as if stretching for something out of reach.

The desert poppies too have begun to tatter and fade. In a few weeks not one will be visible on the ridge. But during their transitory tenure they glow with an almost indecent exuberance, brilliantly orange, out in the open sunshine amid the tiny yellow starflowers and pale purple heron's bills.

Occasionally an African daisy lurks within a poppy patch. These plants, favorites of local urbanites, are exotic imports, planted in flower gardens in Mesa and Apache Junction. Like native poppies, daisies produce fluorescent orange flowers after winter rains (or suburban waterings). Whenever I find one growing wild, I carefully uproot the intruder daisy and leave the dying plant to return whatever nutrients it has stolen from the desert.

Introduced species such as the African daisy have a long history of doing damage to the natural communities of plants and animals they invade. For various reasons, a few plants and animals have been able to exploit environments in which they did not evolve, and sometimes the result is the extinction of species endemic to the area into which the intruder exotics were purposefully or accidentally introduced. Extinctions have been most notable on isolated islands, such as the Hawaiian chain, which has been subjected to a veritable Noah's ark of imports.

The effect of introduced species on the fauna and flora of the Sonoran Desert has been less obviously dramatic, but it has been substantial nonetheless. Most of the common grasses that flourish in Sonoran soil during the spring are European in origin. They became established accidentally long ago in the course of moving livestock between the continents. But a host of non-native grasses have been deliberately introduced as well in an unending effort to satisfy the rapacious appetites of the hordes of cattle and sheep that we have inflicted on the desert. The U.S. Forest Service, for example, has introduced weeping love grass, an African perennial, into various portions of the Tonto National Forest, the better to feed the exotic livestock of the area.

Other imports in the desert include non-native palo verdes, introduced as ornamentals for urban landscaping, that have escaped into desert fringes. Starlings in the past forty years have reached Arizona and now smugly occupy prime nesting holes in saguaro cacti, evicting the Gila woodpeckers and elf owls that would otherwise use these limited nest sites.

Honeybees are yet another exotic that belong in Europe, Asia, and Africa, but not here. They would not be here were it not for beekeepers and the honey industry. William Schaffer and his colleagues at the University of Arizona have clear evidence that honeybees compete head-on with native bees for at least some kinds of nectar. By removing two hives of domestic honeybees from a desert area rich in flowering agaves, Schaffer's crew was able to show an extremely sharp increase in the number of native bees and wasps foraging at the agaves. But then as feral honeybees found the flowering agaves, the number of individuals of native species, which had reached at least ten times the baseline level, began to fall back quickly under the onslaught of these efficient competitors.

Native bees, of which there are many species, do not form large colonies, nor do they share information about food sources as do the members of a honeybee colony. The famous dances of worker honeybees convey data on the distance and direction to a superior source of pollen and nectar. When a worker returns to her hive, she dances on the vertical face of the honeycomb and her movements indicate to those bees that follow her in what direction and how far they must travel to reach the food source that stimulated the worker to dance. After attending to a recruiter, a worker may fly out directly by herself to the location advertised by the successful forager in the dark, buzzing interior of the hive. If she likes what she finds, she too will dance upon her return. This can lead to a rapid buildup of recruits at a good food source, and it makes the honeybees formidable competitors in the exploitation of the temporary riches of the desert.

The same system of communication enables a scout bee to announce the location of a new homesite when she returns to her swarm after a successful search. Her dances may stimulate other workers to leave the swarm to inspect a potential new home for the colony. If they are stimulated by the quality of the site, they too may dance upon their return, attracting still more recruits to the spot. Usually several sites are announced by different scouts, and in one sense, the discoverers compete to attract others to the various possibilities. The best location is one that is of an appropriate size for the swarm, safe and sheltered, and reasonably distant from the hive that the queen abandoned. A superior location will eventually be inspected by an ever-increasing number of recruits, who will dance longer and more vigorously than workers returning from defective places. When the large majority of dancers all direct their colony mates to the same spot, the swarm will depart en masse to this location. A swarm going over the peaktop sounds like a whirlwind rushing past.

One has to admire the honeybee for the sophistication of its behavior, even if the animal is an import. But the very skill with which a colony finds new homes and communally gathers the best food resources threatens the native solitary bees. Each solitary bee female lives by herself, without a dedicated retinue of thousands of daughter-workers, and she must single-handedly gather supplies for her brood cells, which are often placed at the end of an underground burrow. The female lays an egg on the provisions in each cell and then seals the nest, never to see her progeny.

Both honeybees and native species visit flowering desert annuals because they provide nectar and pollen in return for pollination services. Currently it is far more common to see a honeybee blundering about a poppy or dangling from a fiddleneck than it is to see a native bee at work at these plants.

There is at least one species of solitary bee with a special fondness for fiddleneck flowers, a chunky black insect about the size of a honeybee but more compact and with a much noisier, more energetic flight. As it zips from plant to plant, sometimes hovering for a moment in front of a blossom, it announces its presence with authority. But the rarity of its cocky buzz in comparison to the softer hum of the more numerous honeybees merely serves to underline its current subordination to the social newcomer.

I know of no evidence, however, that links the advent of honeybees in the Sonoran Desert with the extinction of any native bee. Perhaps this is simply because honeybees reached Arizona about four hundred years ago and no one in the years shortly thereafter studied the impact of their arrival. For the same reasons, no one knows whether desert annuals have suffered in any way as a result of alterations in the pollinator community. Without doubt there are numerous species of native annuals alive and well today in the desert.

This is fortunate, for there is much to admire about the special relationship of these plants to their environment. Over the millennia, selection has favored those variants within ancestral populations that made germination of their seeds dependent upon winter rainfall. Winter storms are reasonably predictable over the whole of the desert, but it often happens that some areas receive more rain than others. It is also possible to have one dry winter after another. In the springs succeeding such dry winters, the poppies and lupines, mariposa lilies and goldfields will not appear. But after a winter in which a series of Pacific storms has watered the desert, seeds that have lain dormant for years will germinate and the desert will erupt in color in March and April. On barren rocky hillsides, poppies form patches of orange that can be seen for miles, and lupines create blankets of blue that attract pollinators from afar. Once the seeds of annuals germinate, the plants grow quickly, taking advantage of an abundance of open space between the larger perennial shrubs and trees where the warm sunshine can easily reach them, fostering speedy growth and reproduction. But with their modest root systems and large water-losing leaves and flowers, they could not survive the heat and lack of rainfall of the approaching summer. Instead they have evolved to flower quickly and set seed promptly, gambling all on the possibility that sufficient ground moisture will persist in the spring to enable them to mature and to produce seeds in a few weeks. These seeds may lie dormant for years before repeating the cycle.

What a pleasure it is for an enthusiast of biological diversity that there are two such radically different patterns of life history in desert plants: the small annuals that lead adult lives of such flamboyance and brevity and the enduring perennials that seek to overcome the desert at its worst.

Brittlebush

A blustery wind propels streaked clouds over the ridge while a line of showers advances on Four Peaks. Those poppies still in flower are furled tightly against the weather. A lesser goldfinch clings like an uncertain acrobat to a swaying ocotillo stalk, and far overhead a band of swallows flutters darkly in the cold wind.

Only the brittlebush with its bright flowers defies the darkness of the day. Even as the number of flowering poppies has declined, the peak period of brittlebush blossom has arrived. Two- and three-foot-high explosions of yellow ornament the ridge along its entire length and breadth. The daisylike flowers remain open throughout the day in all kinds of weather, in sensible expectation of a return of sunshine.

Brittlebush is a small perennial shrub that, like the desert annuals, responds to winter rainfall. Plants (and animals) that live in extremely variable environments are not automatons programmed to proceed blindly through a life cycle, come what may. Instead they are able to alter their tactics in response to current conditions. When the rains have been generous, brittlebush responds by producing a mass of water-transpiring flowers, but if the storms do not come, the plant will reduce or eliminate its investment in reproduction that year. The capacity to flower is in turn almost certainly related to the plant's allocation of resources to the production of leaves.

For much of the year the plant looks parched and withered as it waits and waits beneath the brutal summer sun, its outer leaves white with hairs that scatter and reflect the fierce light. But in the cooler months, if there has been rain, the plant generates new leaves — larger, greener, and less hairy — that collect the winter sun's more manageable energy. This energy is channeled eventually into the production of a host of thin, yellowish green stalks that rise a foot or more above the leafy mass of the plant. At this stage brittlebush looks like a surrealistic green pincushion with elongate pins stuck in it everywhere. At the tip of each stalk is a greenish yellow bud that in due course opens into a radiant flower. A plant that is in excellent condition changes during the blooming season from a nondescript pale green shrub into a hemisphere of yellow petals. Because brittlebush is a very common plant that flowers synchronously over broad areas, it transforms entire hillsides, which exchange their customary coat of green and brown and gray for a temporary cloak of sunny yellow.

A host of insects celebrate, including aphids that line the flower stalks like teenagers at a soda fountain to siphon the nutrients traveling to the flowers. The consumers of aphids, ladybird beetle larvae, wander along the stalks, looking like miniature gila monsters, their bodies bejeweled with dark blue and reddish tubercules. Syrphid flies nervously hover and zip from flower to flower in search of nectar. A little moth caterpillar consumes the petals surreptitiously, having previously cut off and placed whole petals on the hooked hairs of its back, hiding itself beneath its meal. With its petal camouflage in place, it can safely enjoy its aesthete's feast, hidden from the sharp eyes of verdins and black-tailed gnatcatchers that would make a meal of the moth caterpillar itself.

Brittlebush flowers are also food for a meloid (blister) beetle, *Lytta magister*. This insect gourmand makes no effort to hide from birds or anything else, but in full view of the world mows its way ravenously through flower petal after flower petal, producing an almost continuous dribble of pasty yellow excrement from its other end. Meloid beetles are large insects whose soft, engorged bodies and slippery flexible wing covers give them an appearance very unlike the typically crisp, neat, and trim look of most beetles. But despite their unseemly feeding habits and decadently flabby bodies, the beetles have a strikingly attractive coloration — jet-black wing covers, red-orange head and thorax, and a black and red abdomen. The beetle's color combination makes it highly conspicuous when it perches on the flower stalks of brittlebush. Its apparent disdain for predators is fully justified because when it is molested, the beetle can produce toxic globules by "bleeding" droplets of fluid at the knee joints of one or more legs. The liquid contains cantharidin, which causes irritation and eventual blistering of a human handler's skin. Cantharidin is also known as Spanish fly and is erroneously supposed to be an aphrodisiac. If eaten, it causes damage to the internal digestive tract and to the urogenital system when it is excreted.

Humans are generally little inclined to consume beetles, and therefore, can hardly have been the agents of selection responsible for the evolution of the cantharidin-secreting capacity of blister beetles. The major natural enemies of blister beetles are probably insectivorous birds, lizards, and perhaps certain ants and other carnivorous insects. Some of these predators are not deterred by the defenses of blister beetles; several times I have seen ash-throated flycatchers capture a flying beetle, return to a perch, pound the victim against a limb, and consume it with apparent relish. But others are put off by the taste of the cantharidin-containing liquid, which also has a most repulsive odor. James Carrel and Thomas Eisner have shown experimentally that cantharidin is a feeding repellent for some insects that might otherwise attack meloids. (They note that they were not willing to test the taste of cantharidin themselves because they had read a report in the early French literature that ingested cantharidin causes "érections douloureuses et prolongées.")

The fact that cantharidin tastes bad to some of the blister beetle's enemies means that a predator need not consume a beetle in its entirety before regretting its decision. This benefits both the predator, whose internal organs are spared a massive dose of cantharidin, and the beetle, which is spared death temporarily.

The beetle's bright coloring reminds once-educated predators (birds and lizards are very good at learning to avoid foods that taste bad) of the unpleasant consequences of handling this inedible species. Evil-tasting, toxic, noxious, and stinging insects (and other animals) are often marked with black and orange, or black and yellow, or black and red. Apparently these color combinations make it easier for certain predators to remember a previous bad experience with a food item and so avoid it thereafter. If so, warning coloration offers protection to those animals that have it.

Thus the petal-covered moth larva and meloid beetle adult have taken two very different evolutionary routes in their battles with predators, the one perfecting a method of camouflaging its tasty body, the other advertising its blisteringly toxic properties for all the world to see and avoid.

The distribution patterns of the two species are related to the separate ways in which they thwart predators. The moth larva is highly dispersed, perhaps in part simply because it is a relatively rare animal. If you find one larva, you are unlikely to find another nearby. Typically, members of camouflaged species do not cluster together. Bird predators learn quickly to zero in on the key visual cues that give away the presence of insects they enjoy as meals. If cryptically colored caterpillars gathered together, it would pay a keen-eyed cactus wren or verdin, once it had found that prey, to search carefully through a bush for more. By keeping apart from its fellows, an edible caterpillar reduces the chance that it will become the sort of prey for which a predator searches specifically. Without a particular search image in mind, a bird may be more likely to overlook a cryptic prey, much to the benefit of the prey.

The meloid, too, is not particularly common, and vast patches of brittlebush contain not a single blister beetle. But if you happen to encounter one, the odds are excellent that dozens or hundreds will decorate nearby bushes with their flaccid black bodies. Warningly colored insects often form conspicuous groups. If one of their companions serves as an unpleasant lesson for a predator, the other members of the aggregation can gain, for the predator will immediately apply what it has just learned and avoid them. A dispersed solitary individual is more likely to encounter a naïve enemy that might kill or disable it before its toxins have taken effect. Thus hunting pressure from inexperienced predators may favor noxious meloids (and other insects) that are attracted to other members of their species.

The blatant aggregations of blister beetles typically form on mountain ridges and peaks during the brittlebush season. Flying upwind, the big beetles come swooping in, their elytral covers raised like black angel wings to permit the functional, transparent underwings to power their flight. One can often watch a beetle zigzagging in the wind, as if it were tracking an odor plume coming from other beetles already in the area. Eventually airborne beetles come in for a crash landing. And crash they do, but, like insect Evel Knievels, they are quickly on their feet after thumping down and soon join their companions in a feast of brittlebush flowers.

Thus the blister beetle, like the tarantula hawk and great purple hairstreak, is attracted to conspicuous landmarks. Once on a hilltop the beetles not only feed, they copulate with abandon. About thirty percent of the individuals in a cluster are *in copula* at any moment during the life of the aggregation, not that they permit mating to interfere with a good meal. A male and female go from flower to flower in a continuous search for more food during the twenty-four-hour period in which they are copulating. During their union, the male and female face in opposite directions, attached by the male's elaborate penis, which has harpoonlike spines along its shaft.

Although blister beetles are hilltopping insects, their mating system differs sharply from that of the tarantula hawks and hairstreaks. Male beetles exhibit no territorial defense of landmark waiting sites; instead they attempt to locate receptive females promptly. Once successful, a male dallies with his partner for a period hundreds of times longer than that of a male tarantula hawk with his female.

Why has male reproductive strategy diverged so dramatically among these insects? Earlier we predicted that males should employ the most profitable route available to them in the unconscious competition to fertilize as many females (and eggs) as possible. Female meloids do occur in conspicuous clusters in certain places, unlike female tarantula hawks or hairstreaks. If male beetles defended a hilltop waiting site (landmark defense) or a patch of brittlebush (resource defense), they would almost certainly be less likely to encounter females than males that directly searched for the odor cues associated with aggregations of feeding females.

But once having found a multitude of meloids, why don't males compete to monopolize locations containing several females, thereby assuring themselves access to several mates? Unlike the tarantula hawk and hairstreak, whose females apparently are available in small numbers over a long period (males of both species appear on hilltops for several months), the meloid has a much shorter overall breeding period, no more than one month, and any one aggregation is highly ephemeral. Typically the beetles fly in one day, increase in numbers for the next day or two, leapfrogging along the ridge while ravaging the local plants, and disband on the fourth or fifth day. There is only a short spell when defense of an area would yield matings for a territorial male. The absence of territoriality during this time may stem in part from the poor maneuverability of a flying male (it is hard to imagine precisely how one of these creatures could patrol a territory effectively). And because each copulation lasts so long, a male could hope at best for a couple of matings during the life of an aggregation.

Any investment in territorial patrolling would therefore produce a poor reward for the time and energy expended; the time lost in defending a site would be especially costly because there is such a short interval in which the male can find and inseminate a female. Thus male meloids eschew territory defense and instead try to outrace rivals for receptive partners by moving from one female to the next, courting each in turn with elaborate antennal strokings until finally a female acquiesces.

If matings lasted one minute instead of twenty-four hours, a male would be able to inseminate more than one or two females per aggregation. Why do the beetle copulations last for such a very long time? We have no definitive answer to this question yet, but evolutionary logic can suggest some tenable hypotheses. A male's impact on the evolution of his species really depends on the number of eggs he actually fertilizes, not the number of females with which he mates. In most insects, including our meloid friends, females possess a sperm-storage organ (the spermatheca). Typically, the sperm-storage structure is a small sac at the end of a tubular connection to the female's reproductive tract. During copulation, sperm are either placed directly within the spermatheca by a long-penised male or else they migrate there under their own power. There is no guarantee, however, that what goes into the spermatheca will exit to fertilize eggs. When a female insect lays her eggs, they pass down the oviduct into her reproductive tract; as they move past the spermathecal duct, the female somehow permits an appropriate quantity of sperm to exit from the spermatheca to fertilize the eggs. A female generally receives far more sperm than she needs to fertilize a lifetime's production of eggs, particularly if she mates with more than one male. The usual rule among insects is that when a female copulates with more than one male before ovipositing, the last male enjoys a major reproductive advantage over those that precede him. If a female mates once and then copulates again, and if she uses the second male's sperm to fertilize all her eggs, her first partner will leave no surviving descendants by this mate.

How can a male blister beetle ensure that his own sperm will fertilize the eggs his mate lays? One solution is to extend the duration of copulation, only releasing the female when it would be to her advantage to oviposit rather than accept another copulation. Perhaps this is what happens with the beetle. If we assume that mated females depart to deposit their eggs elsewhere after they have acquired enough food, then by keeping a mate tied up for a day or two while she forages gluttonously, a male can increase the probability that she will leave the aggregation soon after he releases her. This will improve his chances of fertilizing all her eggs.

One rather weak way to test this hypothesis would be to predict that females who were prematurely separated from a first partner would mate again. Unsentimental researchers can arrange to interrupt copulations, although the male and female genitalia are so tightly interlinked that considerable tugging is required to pull a pair apart. I have marked some of the separated females and found a few *in copula* with a new male the next day.

This result is at least consistent with the notion that males that copulate quickly with their females run a substantial risk of their partners mating again, with another male. The prediction that sperm supersedence will occur in double matings remains to be tested. Even if this were established, one would still have to demonstrate that the average number of egg fertilizations achieved from one or two prolonged copulations exceeds that derived from a greater number of shorter matings. This would be challenging work, but it has been done for some other insects, so it is not an impossible task.

Each perennial brittlebush on the hilltops will probably experience several unwelcome encounters with blister beetles during its lifetime. The loss of its yellow flowers reduces a plant's chances of producing descendants that year while fueling the beetle's machinery, creating eggs that (when fertilized by a strategically adept male) may produce beetles that will come next year to hinder the plant's reproductive effort once again in an ongoing cycle of conflicting interests. Long may the battle between beetle and plant continue on Usery Ridge.

Desert Tortoise

This morning I startle a pale gray racer, and it startles me. The snake slides forward a few feet, hesitates, and then shoots straight ahead for a large flat rock. With consummate smoothness, it glides into a small circular opening between rock and soil and is gone.

Today I continue on past the peaktop, down the descending ridge to the south and then up and down on a generally ascending roller-coaster route featuring two steep climbs that will remove the spring from anyone's step. A young black-throated sparrow flushes from the base of a bursage bush and flies on inexperienced wings to a thicket of palo verde. Its presumptive parents chirp in alarm, the male perched on a staghorn cactus, wings aflutter. He is the perfect desert sparrow, a warm gray back, buffy brown wash on his sides, and black-patched face and throat.

The impromptu trail begins its second heart-pounding, throat-parching rise. Tarantula hawk males scan the horizon from the tops of palo verdes, while large black syrphid flies hover and swirl against the blue sky. Giant boulders protrude from the face of the mountain, and saguaros stand on guard among them. From the highest point, a panorama of great variety presents itself: to the east across the Salt River rises Red Mountain, a butte of totally different geology from Usery Ridge; Apache Junction and Mesa lie to the south, a continuous sea of houses and lawns; Phoenix and Tempe are far to the west; Four Peaks and the desert dominate the north.

Amid this jumbled mosaic of desert, mountain, river, and city, one feature instantly draws the eye: a white line, monumental in scale yet visually simple, that runs straight for miles before turning in a clean angle to run again single-mindedly to the next bend. This is the main canal of the Central Arizona Project (CAP), bisecting Arizona with the precision of a scalpel cut, slicing eastward from the Colorado River, hundreds of miles away, to Phoenix and then southeast toward Tucson.

On the top of the mountain, far from the multi-billion-dollar canal, a desert tortoise smaller than my hand ambles across the gravel. Its chunky armored legs move to their own measured rhythm. Its shell has not lost the yellow-orange bands and ridged texture that will melt to a smooth, dull gray with age. The tortoise will deal with its environment through evolved design rather than seek to deny the desert its due.

The young tortoise is an anomaly, the only youngster I have seen in five springs of desert walking. I resist the urge to pick up the little turtle — the roundness of a desert tortoise's shell and its docility are all too inviting. As many as 20,000 now live imprisoned in the backyards of California homes alone. Thousands more have been flattened, inadvertently or deliberately, by cars and off-road vehicles. Others have been used for target practice. No doubt some died when they fell into an empty CAP canal during the time it was being constructed; currently some may find their way into the now water-filled canal as it supplies the real estate and agricultural interests of Phoenix and Tucson.

The walls of the canal rise steeply some twenty feet or so from the bottom of the channel. A deep, narrow canal reduces the rate of evaporation, which is monumental in any case, and the nearly vertical walls facilitate the rapid movement of Colorado River water eastward along the canal. For years, portions of the unfinished canal lay across Arizona like a huge pit trap into which tumbled beetles and deer, rattlesnakes and racers; once in the canal, these unfortunates died of thirst or heat, baked by the sun that shone indifferently on the concrete trap. Now that water flows through the entire canal, those that descend into the channel drown, although fortunately the waterway is fenced for most of its length.

The difficulties faced by tortoises in the past have already reduced them to remnant populations living in rocky mountainous terrain, such as Usery Ridge, places unsuitable for houses, agriculture, freeways, or water projects. A tortoise must survive some twelve to twenty years before it is old enough to attempt to reproduce. Females lay small clutches of three to seven eggs, one clutch per year. Those few eggs not discovered by Gila monsters and coyotes hatch into minute animals that are vulnerable to predators for several years. These problems have always been with the tortoise, but in the past an animal that reached adulthood could expect to live thirty to seventy years more. But now, the fragmentation of their habitat, the complete loss of much lowland desert, the pressures of competition from domestic livestock, and the removal of countless numbers of full-grown animals by human collectors all conspire to reduce the effective life expectancy of adults in the wild. This may make it impossible for the reptiles to replace themselves in most areas, for an animal may not have thirty, forty, or fifty years in which to produce a replacement or two. The prognosis is not good for the desert tortoise.

In order to learn more about the biology of the animal, graduate students under the guidance of Robert Ohmart have placed miniature radio transmitters on the backs of some individuals. By tracking these animals they have found that adults have a large home range of about forty or fifty acres with which they seem highly familiar. When temperatures are suitable, tortoises travel about a half-mile (as the raven flies) per day, moving about a circuit that often leads them back eventually to the very place from which they had started some days previously. On warm spring and fall days they lumber through the desert, feeding on the grasses and annuals that have not already been consumed by grazing cattle. But during the ferocious heat of summer they retire to deep dens dug into the banks of washes. In the wintertime a tortoise may simply sit beneath a shrub like a stone, tucked in, conserving moisture accumulated in the few months suitable for feeding. The reptile possesses an oversized bladder in which it stores useful water derived from the plants it consumes.

Once in my ignorance I picked up a large tortoise wandering on the ridge on a late spring day. It urinated copiously on me. This seems to be a reaction of manhandled turtles, presumably a last-ditch, desperate attempt to startle or repel the handler, which in nature likely would be a turtle predator. The desert tortoise's stream of reddish urine surprised me, although I had no intention of consuming the beast. Only later did I learn that the loss of fluids might well have been as fatal for the animal as if I had eaten or driven over it. I hope that tortoise was able to recharge its supply of stored water in time to survive the dog days of summer.

To see a tortoise with wrinkled neck and solemn eyes, moving like an animated rock, is an essential part of the experience of the desert. The removal of even a single adult extinguishes a presence that was meant to persist for years to come and snuffs out a prehistoric spark of life in a spartan environment where life, so hard-won, should be celebrated.

Hedgehog Cacti

On the hillside far across the plain above the Salt River, the largest fountain in the world erupts, spewing a gigantic geyser in the air. The descending spray drifts downwind to water a vast surrounding greensward, an appropriately desert-defiant symbol of Fountain Hills, a huge development of tract homes that has been cut into the Sonoran landscape to the west of Usery Ridge. Paved roads meander in self-conscious loops and circles through the artificial greenery favored by eastern and midwestern transplants to Arizona. To accommodate their clients, developers here carefully scrape away all but remnant vestiges of desert vegetation, a lone saguaro here, a pathetically isolated palo verde tree there. Into the erased desert go roads, homes, Bermuda grass, or green gravel lawns with eucalyptus and oleanders to replace the acacias and ironwoods. Occasionally the residents of Fountain Hills report a peccary or a coyote straying across terrain that must seem as exotic to the animals as Katmandu would to the humans that occupy the development.

Usery Ridge basks in the sun, light-years from Fountain Hills. A Gambel's quail calls in the distance. The number of palo verdes occupied by territorial tarantula hawks has grown from one or two to nine today. Patrolling intruders sail up and down the ridge, clashing with each resident in turn, filling the air with black wasp chases and graceful spiral flights. Near palo verde #17 a hedgehog cactus blooms. The cylindrical little hedgehog cactus usually grows in clumps, four to eight small arms rising from a recumbent trunk, looking rather like a collection of upright zucchini squashes densely covered with brown- and white-tipped spines. Plump flower buds, green with white and tan stripes, have been growing at the tips of hedgehog arms. Some have now burst open, revealing rich red-purple flowers. Each flower encloses a brilliant velvet-green stamen and a mass of straw-yellow anthers. A patch of hedgehog cacti in flower looks something like a baby porcupine carrying a cluster of red tulips on its back.

The hedgehog cactus near palo verde #17 began blooming on April 9 but now, only a week later, most of its flowers, once vibrant and glossy, have faded and burned beneath the sun. The spent flowers look like tufts of pale reddish crepe paper twisted into place. One freshly opened flower, however, still radiantly announces the delights of spring in the desert. A small yellow *Perdita* bee, a male, perches head-down on a lustrous petal. His antennae twitch as he awaits the arrival of a mate.

In Fountain Hills honeybees fly, droning from one American Beauty to the next, while hoses water the roses endlessly.

Many occupants of Fountain Hills have opted for desert landscaping, a growing trend in the American Southwest as the cost of lawn watering rises and more people become aware of the sensible pleasures of owning drought-tolerant plants. A hedgehog cactus loses water at the rate of six-tenths of a milligram per square centimeter of surface area for each hour of exposure at eighty-five degrees, a rate that is a fraction of that for organisms not adapted to desert conditions. (A 150-pound man's rate of water loss under the same circumstances is thirty times higher.) Ironically, the desert landscaping trend poses a different threat to native vegetation, one a bit more subtle than that posed by a developer's bulldozers or by the bullets of desert marksmen, but just as devastating.

Hedgehog cacti offer a case in point. Because of their showy flowers, they are very much in demand for desert-landscaping projects. As a result, in some federal and state-owned lands, populations of hedgehog cacti have been depleted by professional thieves who sell illegally removed plants to nurseries or individuals. A permit is required to remove cactus from any place in Arizona, although permits are easily secured if the plants grow on private property. But the state provides only a handful of men to protect native vegetation growing on ninety thousand square miles of Arizona. So thieves operate with impunity, digging out the shallow-rooted hedgehogs with a few thrusts of a shovel, leaving behind a fresh scar in the ground and a few unwanted, broken fragments of cactus.

It must be a long, long time before a new hedgehog replaces one abducted to dispense springtime cheerfulness in a front yard in Phoenix, Scottsdale, or Paradise Valley. The establishment of a seedling of any of the perennial desert plants seems to be an extraordinarily rare event, and so populations of these species are composed of ancient survivors, barely growing, unchanging from year to year. The damage done by cactus rustlers cannot be repaired; they reduce the diversity of the desert and rob it of its color for a lifetime, leaving the desert impoverished for us all.

Varmint Hunters and Other Gunners

Striding along the ridge from the south, a varmint hunter and his companion puff their way up the peaktop. Each carries a rifle, and the varmint hunter owns a revolver as well. On his head sits a dirty leather Confederate campaign hat saturated with sweat and grease. I am armed with an insect net and a backpack. Little is said about what I might be doing. The varmint hunter wants to talk about shooting coyotes. He had seen one. They had gotten off some shots. Had I heard them? I had. They had missed. He is cheerful about it. Coyotes are hard to kill.

I once saw a coyote in the very spot where the varmint hunter and I now converse. The coyote came along the slope in a straight line, as though he knew precisely where he was headed. He did not see me but went smartly down and across the saddle between my peak and the higher one to the south before disappearing into the gullies and broken land in the distance. He was thin and his pale brown coat was scruffy, but there was a jauntiness, a confidence, in his light step that was a pleasure to see.

Many more gunners than coyotes come to the Usery area. The large gravel pit excavated by the highway department draws weekend shooters like a magnet. Bulls-eye targets, shattered bottles, cans shredded by hails of bullets, and expended cartridges litter the pit. Bullets have wounded and gouged all manner of plants in the vicinity of the shooting range, especially the tempting saguaros with their almost-human outlines. The gunners fan out from the gravel pit to travel up washes or walk the desert, discharging their firearms with abandon at man-made and natural targets. On weekends in the spring one could be forgiven for imagining bands of partisans in the hills, engaged in the preliminaries of World War III.

The echoing crashing report of a high-powered rifle dominates the desert, which otherwise is one of the quietest places imaginable. Studies by Bayard Brattstrom and M. C. Bondelo have shown that the noise level in desert habitats rarely exceeds forty decibels, a level characteristic of a library. The pulse of noise produced by gunshots may reach 160 decibels, a sound-pressure level thousands upon thousands of times louder than the background noise, an intensity equivalent to that produced by a jet plane on takeoff at close range.

A bullet passing overhead greatly multiplies the tenseness of a day punctuated by gunfire. Whining long shots and tumbling ricochets are now part of the desert experience on Usery Ridge on far too many days.

There is little to be done except to take cover as best one can. Once I had to return to my parking place near the gravel pit when it was occupied by gunners whose bullets had pierced the air above the ridge from time to time. Using side ridges and gullies, I had an uneventful descent until I crested the bank of a wash. Through the feathery branches of an intervening palo verde I saw, some distance away, a man with a large black revolver. The revolver pointed at me and discharged explosively sending a bullet a few feet from my head.

My shouted protest, full of fear and outrage, prompted the pistol-packer and his companions to reply that, hey, they were there first and I should go elsewhere to shoot. My would-be killer was under the mistaken impression, albeit an entirely reasonable one given his experience with other visitors to the area, that the only reason anyone would be there would be to exercise his firearms.

In the state of Arizona one may not shoot from a car or across a roadway. Doubtless there are a few other restrictions, but in general the desert is fair game. This is an unfortunate policy, but I am not sure that I wish to discuss the philosophy of the matter with my gun-toting opponents near Usery Ridge. For the moment I would be satisfied if they would be kind enough to shoot directly into something solidly inanimate, leaving the odd coyote and me to walk the ridge with a modest amount of confidence.

Collared Peccaries

My son and I descend an outlying ridge and gradually make our way to one of the main gullies feeding a major wash that runs through the plain to the west. The arroyo has cut a deep narrow trough in the ridge; it is perfectly dry today and only the patterns of sandy deposits among the rocks reveal that water sometimes rushes through to the desert below.

The high walls of the feeder gully constrict at a spot where solid rock has been carved by past flows. Below a dry waterfall a yard high, the main wash begins in a little amphitheater densely filled with rabbit brush and thorny scrub. From here on the wash grows quickly in width, and the eroded banks, held in place by brittlebush, mesquite, and palo verde, gradually lower as the angle of descent of the wash lessens.

On the right-hand side of the bushy basin, solid bedrock forms a slanted wall. As winter rains percolate downhill through looser, more gravelly soil, they reach this impenetrable layer of bedrock. Water slowly inches underground along the rocky layer, just surfacing at this point where bedrock and sandy wash coincide. A tiny pool, or seep, no larger than my hand, rests in a depression shaded by desert shrubbery.

A pair of black-tailed gnatcatchers weave their way through a jojoba bush, black eyes peering, tails trailing. Their thin querulous calls wheeze from the vegetation.

My son and I have come to look for peccary, desert pigs that visit the seep. A few days ago a small band trotted out of the brush by the pool and went up over a rise toward a maze of washes and rocky outcrops to the south. Today the band is nowhere to be seen.

As we drop over the rock ledge into the basin to check the seep, a single large peccary bursts from dense chaparral a few yards away. Its bristle, snort, and stamp turn our complacent approach into an undignified retreat. As my son and I retrace our steps with celerity, I can almost feel the pig's canines cutting into my legs with surgical precision. But the many stories of peccary ferocity have doubtless been inflated by hunters seeking to justify the afflictions that they so enthusiastically impose on this species. Our peccary, like most others, is harmless; he truculently stands his ground for a moment before turning to leave the wash in search of a spot less visited by humans.

Collared peccaries (or javelinas) live primarily in tropical South and Central America, where two other species of peccary also occur. From this we can infer that collared peccaries evolved in wet tropical woodlands. Some authors believe that only in the last million years or so, just a flicker in geological time, have collared peccaries extended their range into the arid southwestern United States, and only in the last century have they become reasonably common in Arizona.

In some respects Arizona peccaries bear the imprint of their tropical past, for they lack many of the exceptionally specialized water-conserving adaptations of other desert animals. Instead they rely primarily on such simple devices as feeding at night and resting in the shade during the day throughout the summer. But they possess other attributes that help prevent water loss and overheating. As summer approaches, the pigs exchange their coarse dark winter fur for a paler coat, the better to reflect sunlight during the scorching months of the year. Should a peccary be forced to go awhile without water, it can reduce the volume of urine it excretes by ninety percent, thus saving the body fluids on which its survival depends until it reaches a secure source of moisture. But the animals need water regularly; they know where and when the fickle seeps flow and use their dainty hooves to scrape away the sand, deepening the pools.

Although their physiology has not been strongly shaped by the pressures of the desert, peccaries nevertheless do well in Sonoran habitats. In part their success may stem from the economy of their diets. Despite their relationship to pigs, their bodies are wiry, thin, and laterally compressed, all backbone and muscle and not a trace of slovenly fat. On thin legs, they fastidiously pick their way among the cholla cactus and dried brittlebush, stopping here and there to feed leisurely on the red fruits of hedgehog cactus and the pads of prickly pear. Broken cactus spines, implanted during earlier meals, project from their soft and sensitive-looking snouts. To sustain itself solely on prickly pear, an adult needs to consume about three pounds per day, an amount easily secured in many places. The succulent tissues of cacti provide food and water for any animal able to consume them and willing to ignore the intimidating needle-barbed spines of these plants.

Peccaries exhibit another exceptional feature: their extreme sociality. One rarely sees a solitary peccary; the animals habitually associate in fixed bands of five to fifteen members. Perhaps the solo individual that frightened my son and me was an individual in search of a band, or perhaps its group was just over the rise in a neighboring wash. But John Byers and Marc Bekoff, who studied peccaries in the 3-Bar Wildlife Area a short distance from Usery Ridge, found that most individuals remained no more than fifteen feet from one another at all times. The pigs have scent glands on their backs: one peccary will rub the back of a companion with its chin, then the other pig reciprocates, each thereby distributing its scent over the other's coat. Because peccaries have woefully bad eyesight, group cohesion may be maintained by odor signals as well as by certain vocalizations, particularly one called the "low grunt."

The importance of being a member of a tightly knit band doubtless has to do with the ability of herds of peccaries to defend themselves and their young better than solitary animals. If a coyote threatens to snatch a youngster from a group, the juveniles cluster with some adults while other mature peccaries confront the coyote. Peccaries have dangerously sharp canines and are surprisingly agile adversaries; by dealing with enemies in groups the pigs greatly raise the risk of injury for a predator, encouraging it to go elsewhere. Baby peccaries, although born at an advanced stage of development and capable of following the band within a day or two of birth, are nevertheless tiny and vulnerable. The cooperative sociality of adults in the group must help to protect them.

Cooperative, friendly relations within a band extend even to communal nursing of the young by all the adult females, a most unusual phenomenon. The logic of evolutionary theory suggests that indiscriminate nursing should rarely occur because a female that gives her valuable milk to young other than her own increases the likely reproductive success of another individual while lowering her own capacity to leave descendants. In a population composed of such helpful females, a mutant individual who permitted her young to partake of the largess provided by other females while at the same time "selfishly" restricting her own handouts so as to feed her own young preferentially would seem to have a reproductive advantage. If so, the selfish trait would soon spread and eliminate the indiscriminate nursing alternative.

But this has not happened in collared peccaries. One hypothesis to account for the persistence of altruistic nursing is that peccary bands contain groups of female relatives. Thus a sister might nurse her nephews and nieces, a grandmother might give milk to her grandchildren. Because relatives share a certain proportion of genes inherited from a common ancestor, it is theoretically possible for the genetic basis of altruism that is directed at relatives to spread through a population. An individual's impact on the evolution of its species is really measured by the number of its own genes that it transmits to subsequent generations. Having offspring is the direct way to propagate one's genes. Helping relatives survive to reproduce is an indirect means toward the same end.

Lion prides, which are composed of clusters of female relatives, have also evolved communal nursing. Unfortunately, no one knows whether the females in a band of collared peccaries are relatives, as the selective-altruism hypothesis requires. But biologists have found that band members, although wonderfully tolerant of each other, react with great hostility to outsiders. Observers of peccaries rarely see an individual transfer successfully to a new group, and even when such a transfer does happen, there is generally a period of attack and aggression directed toward the newcomer. This finding is consistent with the notion that females do not transfer benefits willy-nilly, but direct them primarily to the offspring of their genetically similar relatives with whom they have grown up.

Because peccaries are not as easily captured and marked as tarantula hawks or hairstreaks, it may be some time before someone musters the necessary energy and patience needed to test the hypothesis that female peccaries selectively help their relatives. But the question is there, and eventually it will be answered, adding a small but significant dimension to our understanding of the evolution of behavior.

May

Illustration: Spadefoot toad

Gambel's Quail

As April turns to May and temperatures push upward toward the formidable levels of summer, the seep becomes important for a host of animals in addition to peccaries. Honeybees line the margins of the pool for a drink. Upon returning to its hive, a water-laden worker regurgitates a droplet that it holds between proboscis and chin; wings fanning, the worker transforms herself into a miniature but effective evaporative cooler. As a result of workers' efforts, the hive's temperature never exceeds 95 degrees, even though it may be 115 degrees or more on the outside. Although each bee is small, the great numbers of these drinkers may remove more total water than some of the much larger visitors attracted to the seep.

Mourning doves alight in the bare branches of a dead mesquite near the pool and wait and wait, uncertain of their reception at the water's edge. A migrant green-tailed towhee lurks in the scrub on its journey to cooler habitats farther north; it slips from limb to limb, red cap flared and brilliant even in the shade. The forewing of a painted lady lies in the sand of the wash; the butterfly that once owned the wing is now doubtless in the stomach of an ash-throated flycatcher.

Farther down the dry bed of the watercourse the remains of a camp of jojoba pickers disfigures the desert. A group had driven up the wash and changed the oil in their vehicles, leaving the empty cans and old oil behind to stain the sand and taint the air. Cardboard boxes, unused burlap sacks, and dried hulls of thousands of jojoba fruits litter the ground. With the decline of the whaling industry, jojoba seeds have become valuable, for they contain a high-grade oil nearly identical to that produced by sperm whales. Permits are now issued for jojoba seed harvests; at several dollars a pound, a person can make some money from the plant. So the economy of the Tonto National Forest expands to include jojoba in addition to timber, minerals, grazing, and water. A land of multiple uses. A white-winged dove passes overhead. The search for a substitute for sperm whale oil to help conserve the whale may also help speed the degradation of the dove's Sonoran habitat.

Gambel's quail abound in the vicinity of the seep, even in the bushes that border the old camp of jojoba pickers. Everywhere clusters of recently hatched chicks associate with an adult. To walk the wash today is to set off one alarm after another, adults calling with a greater and greater sense of urgency, young scuttling frantically through the underbrush, or flying up in experimental flight, golden brown balls of feathers and dangling legs. Coveys dash for safety up the walls of the wash. The flocks vary enormously, some composed of half-grown chicks, others of chicks so fresh out of the egg that English sparrows would seem to be the larger bird. The quail are numerous now, for each female lays many eggs. But soon many of the chicks whose liveliness now fills the wash will become victims of starvation, heat, coyotes, and Cooper's hawks. In the fall the coveys of survivors will be fewer, and the wash will be a more subdued oasis than it is today.

Unlike collared peccaries, Gambel's quail appear to have evolved for a long time within the demanding environment of the desert, for they exhibit a number of special adaptations to this world. For example, compared to its close relative, the California quail, a bird of wetter habitats than the Sonoran Desert, Gambel's quail conserves water better by producing a more concentrated urine and by dehydrating more slowly when deprived of water. The desert-adaptedness of Gambel's quail also emerges in its ability to make reproduction contingent upon sufficient winter rainfall, as do so many other Sonoran Desert animals and plants. In the spring a quail may leave the relative safety of its winter covey in an attempt to defend a territory and reproduce, or it can remain in the flock and not breed at all. The birds' physiological systems make these decisions for them on the basis of the quality of food they consume in the late winter months. If winter rains have been generous and soil conditions are good, there will be considerable new green growth during this time. New growth contains high-protein, high-quality foods that stimulate the redevelopment of female ovaries and male testes, organs that shrink to mere wisps of tissue when the birds are not breeding. (When a bird is not reproducing, it is greatly advantageous not to have to carry about and maintain heavy gonadal tissues that would only make the bird less agile and more vulnerable in encounters with Cooper's hawks.) But if the key nutrients are absent, as they are in stunted weeds and flowers, reproductive tissues will not develop and the birds will wait for another year.

The adaptive significance of this link between food and reproductive physiology seems straight-forward. An abundance of annuals in February and March means a large seed crop later from grasses and desert perennials as well as good insect production by May, just the time when the young will need a great deal of food if they are to have any chance of survival. The extreme annual variation in food supplies in the late spring has favored birds that do not automatically attempt to reproduce each year but instead behave in a discriminating fashion. Gambel's quail that wait for some chance of success before making the large and risky investment in reproduction seem certain to leave more descendants than genetically different types that try to reproduce in the face of impossible odds.

This hypothesis can be tested by predicting that other desert animals should also postpone reproduction if a key indicator of later food supplies is missing. Sonoran Desert species as unlike the quail as the rufous-winged sparrow and spadefoot toad behave as predicted. Both species require a heavy rainfall to trigger the reproductive process. The sparrow, for example, may begin nesting any time from late May to late July, depending on the time of the first serious storm within this period. Rainfall is needed to produce plant growth upon which insects feed; insects supply the calories and nutrients baby sparrows need to grow to adulthood.

The spadefoot toad spends its nonreproductive period burrowed three feet or more beneath the soil near temporary ponds that fill only after a fierce thunderstorm in the summer monsoon season. Unlike sparrows, the spadefoot toads cannot see or feel rainfall but they can and do hear thunder. When a sufficiently loud storm rouses the toad from its resting place, it tunnels upward to mate and feed for a while in a filled pond before resuming its life of isolation underground.

Desert ponds, once filled with water, come alive with aquatic life upon which toad tadpoles feed. They may succeed in racing through to adulthood during the few weeks before the pond evaporates. If it dries before the metamorphosis of the amphibians is complete, they have nowhere to go. Thus the reproductive success of a buried spadefoot depends greatly on its capacity to discriminate and respond to signals associated with severe rainstorms.

As if the life of a spadefoot were not complicated enough, a new problem may have arisen for those animals unfortunate enough to live in areas traveled by off-road vehicles (ORVs). Tapes of revving motorcycles broadcast above buried captive spadefoot toads in a sand-filled terrarium cause the toads to come to the surface. Thus the unmuffled roar of an ORV, so favored by owners of these machines, is potentially loud enough to mimic the sounds of thunder and trigger the emergence of spadefoots. As ORVs pass over the desert, toads may dig their way up, consuming their stores of energy and water in the process, only to find the desert barren and moistureless. Down they will go again, their odds of survival materially decreased. If the process were repeated frequently enough, it seems certain that the local toads would die without reproducing, their beautiful adaptations short-circuited by a trivial human invention whose only function is to amuse while destroying.

Palo Verde

T he palo verdes on the ridge have begun to flower, a signal of the conclusion of spring. First came the poppies, small but flamboyantly orange; then the shrubby brittlebush, brilliantly yellow; and last the foothills palo verde, with its more subdued yellow flowers whose paleness anticipates the austerity of summer. Like the poppies and brittlebush, palo verdes regulate the production of flowers and seeds in accordance with the pattern of winter rains. In dry years the trees hold back and at most produce scattered patches of blossoms here and there at the tips of their prickly branches, creating a mosaic of green and yellow. In good years, like the spring of 1982, flowers completely covered entire trees, and the desert plains and ridges drowned deliciously beneath a sea of yellow that extended to the horizon. For some unknown reason, the flower show this spring does not match that of 1982, despite ample rainfall during the past winter.

In preparation for flowering, palo verdes discard the minute, water-conserving leaves that grow on their outer twigs, which in turn are supported by an undisciplined mass of green branches and limbs radiating from the short trunk of the tree. The leaves, once green, first turn reddish or yellowish brown and then fall, carrying with them a small amount of nitrogen. Palo verdes are legumes, and the roots of legumes contain certain species of bacteria that have the unusual and valuable capacity to capture nitrogen from the air and fix it in a form usable by the plant. Baked desert soils contain little organic material and less nitrogen. The myriad fallen leaflets, blown by the wind, gather in stony pockets on the desert floor like sea wrack trapped in tide pools. There they decay, creating conditions that may once in a long, long while permit the establishment of a plant colonist — a little thick-skinned fern, or a tuft of resilient moss, or a palo verde seedling.

This year the palo verdes shed only some of their leaves, beginning in early April. On the twigs without leaves, small, hemispheric blue-green buds appeared on thin stalks by the end of the month. By today most of the buds have opened, and the modest yellow flowers announce their supplies of nectar and pollen to the insect world. Beetles, flies, and bees, social and solitary, respond to the announcement. Here and there yellow ambush bugs lurk hidden among the petals, their stiletto beaks poised to pierce a pollinator. Crab spiders in near perfect yellow camouflage also await an unsuspecting meal. A lifeless honeybee sways in the breeze, dangling from the jaws of a spider whose all-but-invisible body blends with the color of the flower in which it rests.

Like so many desert plants, palo verdes are advertisements for adaptation. On a mere six inches of rain a year, they grow slowly but steadily to small tree size, capturing the energy of the sun with little leaves that first appear in late May or early June and are retained until next spring, unless severe drought causes the tree to jettison its leaves. Even leafless palo verdes can photosynthesize with their green-barked trunks and limbs. During a prolonged dry spell, a palo verde may permit some of its limbs to die, dropping the autotomized branches to the ground where they will no longer demand scarce nutrients and water of the tree. But when conditions are favorable, the trees produce a spring profusion of flowers, which in due course give rise to thin green seedpods that look rather like the pods of another legume, garden string beans. Within each pod — and there are often tens of thousands on a single palo verde — one to four small beans form, at first milky green and later, when the pods are mature, dark brown. The quantity of beans produced more or less synchronously by the diffuse forest of palo verdes in the plain below the ridge would surely be uncountable in a good year.

Why are the palo verdes so extravagant in the production of future offspring? Perhaps the circumstances suitable for establishment of a seedling are so rarely met that individual trees gain by producing vast numbers of propagules on the off chance that eventually one or two may accidentally, almost miraculously, reach the microenvironment they need for survival and growth. Only in one year in five have I seen any appreciable number of palo verde seedlings. That year was blessed with several late spring storms, each a statistically improbable event, spaced conveniently at intervals of several weeks. Palo verde seeds from the previous year sprouted everywhere in little depressions, no doubt fertilized by the dead leaves of the mature trees nearby. Seedlings quickly grew to a height of three to four inches. But within a few weeks of the last rains, only a handful survived where once there had been thousands. Most simply disappeared, but here and there the neatly clipped remains of a seedling lay withered in the sun. The young palo verdes apparently made tasty snacks for the many local rodents and rabbits. The odds that a seed will encounter conditions suitable for germination and also live long enough to grow to a reasonable size, one that a jackrabbit cannot demolish in a few bites, must be infinitesimally small. Forrest Shreve, working in 1911 with a stand of palo verdes near Tucson, Arizona, reached a similar conclusion. Of the many seedlings he marked, almost none lived to their third year.

The relentless depredations of herbivores help to explain why flowering and seed set of palo verdes are so highly synchronized in an area. By producing its seeds when other trees are generating theirs, an individual palo verde slightly improves the chances that one of its offspring might be among the chosen few lucky enough to be left by the consumers of young palo verdes. If the total seed crop is large enough, there may be so many seedlings in an area that the plant's consumers are satiated before all the palo verdes have been eaten.

And it is not just palo verde seedlings that are at risk. The seeds are attractively edible too. Many seeds never have a chance to be carried by rivulets of water to a sheltering pocket of soil, but instead are collected and eaten by mice or woodrats or destroyed by bruchid beetles. Two bruchids specialize in eating palo verde seeds. One, *Mimosestes amicus*, attacks young pods, glueing its eggs on the outer surface. When the minute larva hatches, it burrows through the green coat of the pod and works its way into a seed.

There it feasts in comfort, killing the seed. Just before the remainder of the seed turns brown and hard, the adult beetle exits, leaving behind a hollowed-out seed coat and a neat hole in the thin dry husk of the pod.

Through the exit holes made by *M. amicus* enter other, smaller bruchids, *Stator limbatus*, in search of uneaten seeds. These beetles hunt for the larger pods with two or more seeds. If there are whole seeds within a pod, *S. limbatus* oviposits on them and her progeny consume the hardened seeds and go through their developmental cycle within the perforated pod.

Because *S. limbatus* depends on pods with more than one seed, its presence favors the production of one-seed pods by palo verdes. If the tree's only consideration were the material cost of packing seeds, the most efficient system would be to put three or more seeds in each pod. This could be done with a fraction of the covering material needed to produce the same number of seeds with each one in a separate package. But because of the preference of *S. limbatus* for multiseeded pods, trees that have many one-seed packages may actually produce more *surviving* seeds than palo verdes that conserve on packaging to produce a greater number of seeds originally — more than one per pod — but lose most to *S. limbatus* before their seeds mature.

Palo verdes are not without an ally in the battle against bruchids. Just as palo verde seeds attract seed-parasitizing bruchids, so too the eggs of bruchids attract a minute wasp, *Uscana semifumipennis*, that lays her eggs in those of the beetle. Each wasp egg gives rise to a larva that consumes the bruchid egg and emerges in twelve days as an adult from what had been its meal. The wasp can be a major destroyer of bruchids, killing about forty percent of the eggs laid by the two beetles in some trees. Moreover, when the wasp is around, *M. amicus* tends to lay her eggs in pairs, one on top of the other. The cap egg protects the bottom one from the wasp parasite but represents a loss in reproductive potential for the beetle who must lay two eggs in order to have a chance for one to hatch. In the laboratory, in the absence of the wasp, *M. amicus* lays her eggs singly, rather than in pairs, although how she knows the wasp is absent is a mystery.

Even though ninety percent of bruchid eggs die before the larva can penetrate a seed, the proportion of a palo verde's offspring that are lost to beetle predation is formidable. In the early summer a few dried and creased seedpods still hang from the trees. Invariably the hollow seeds in these desiccated husks have a neat circular exit hole that was cut in them by their now departed beetle consumers.

Thus despite their capacity for prolific seed production and long lives, adult trees reproduce very rarely. My trees on Usery Ridge, although small, are probably ancient, though their exact ages are a matter of conjecture. To my astonishment, no one since Forrest Shreve in 1911 has tried to age palo verdes. Shreve's methods revealed that many of the trees he examined were over one hundred years old and some had lived in excess of two hundred years, perhaps to even four hundred years.

The high annual survival rate of well-established palo verdes applies to the ridge population. I know of only two trees that have died and toppled in five years on the study plot. The rest stand so little different from when I first saw them that I can detect no change at all.

Each palo verde is a miracle. It would be wonderful to know the complete life story of even one tree on the ridge, to know what coincidences, accidents, and bits of good fortune kept the bruchids, wood rats, and jackrabbits away. How long did the tree take to grow to its present dimensions? What droughts and winds has it experienced? How many wood-boring cerambycid and buprestid beetles have lived within its limbs without killing it? What has been its annual production of flowers and seeds, and how many of its offspring are alive today, anchored in the unpromising soil of the ridge, facing the uncompromising sun with the confidence of survivors?

Digger Bees

In the floodplain of the Salt River by the Blue Point Bridge, off-road vehicles roar in triumph, having reduced what would otherwise be a beautiful and tranquil location to a mass of open wounds, a crazy quilt of barren eroded tracks crisscrossing the flatland. A three-wheeled motorcycle lurches past, motor in full-throated scream, wheels kicking the sandy clay to a dust that drifts to dull the mesquite leaves and dirty the flowers of palo verdes. The rider's smile is grim; his task is to conquer and reconquer the desert.

A few feet from the passing motorcycle, dozens — hundreds — of large gray bees zoom about in much less noisy circles of their own. From time to time, a bee drops to the ground and walks there for a few seconds before beginning to scrabble in the hard-packed clay. There is an urgency to its digging. The bee's jaws loosen dirt while its forelegs frantically propel soil out of a grow-ing pit. Within minutes a hole accommodates the bee's head and thorax. There is a pause, a buzz, then the digger slowly with-draws and another bee comes scrambling to the surface. In a flash, the digger bee mounts the individual it has released from under the ground and they mate, oblivious of the destruction all around them.

Many close associations exist between plant and animal in the desert, but few are more apparent than the symbiosis between the digger bee and the little foothills palo verde of mountain slopes and the larger blue palo verde of riparian floodplains. In the Phoenix area, the life cycle of the bee intertwines with that of the palo verde. For eleven months of the year, digger bees live under-ground in a suspended state intermediate between larva and adult in the brood cell that its mother constructed and provisioned for it. But just before the first palo verdes begin to bloom, the males complete their metamorphosis, changing from prepupa to pupa and then to adult. The bees then gnaw their way up through six inches or so of desert soil. Once above ground, males dedicate their lives to searching out females.

Although the digger bee qualifies as a solitary bee in the sense that females rear their offspring without assistance from workers, the bees often nest in dense aggregations. The following year, large numbers of males and subsequently an equally large number of females emerge from the soil of a relatively small area. The males cruise within a few inches of the ground between 7:30 and 10:30 each morning, searching all the while for the cues associated with preemergent females. When a male detects the key cues, he descends to excavate a mate that is buried a half-inch or so beneath the surface.

How can males locate future partners who have not yet even emerged? Digger males accomplish this remarkable feat by somehow sensing female scent or pheromone that has percolated through the earth. A searching male sweeps his antennae low over the surface of the ground once he has landed, and before he settles on a digging spot. As he digs, his antennae also constantly monitor the excavation site. This is indirect evidence that female detection requires a sense of smell. A direct demonstration of the role olfaction plays in this task involved an experiment in which I buried moribund male and female digger bees as well as the bodies of deceased honeybees and wasps. Male digger bees promptly located all the hidden insects and dug them up.

The experiment reveals first that a buried female need not be moving or making noise of any sort to be located. Odor cues alone suffice for her location. Second, male diggers do not make fine discriminations but apparently respond to any discrepancy in the odor patterns coming from soil that might be associated with an underground insect. In nature, most large insects residing a short distance beneath the soil in digger-bee habitat would be virgin females whose excavation rewards a male profoundly. But even under natural conditions, males sometimes make mistakes and dig up a late-emerging male of their species, always a disappointment for the digger. Males will even occasionally uncover a member of another species, such as the meloid beetle, *Tegrodera aloga*, that is in the process of emerging from a brood cell whose digger-bee contents it had parasitically consumed. (Meloid females lay their eggs on the flowers of palo verdes. When an egg hatches, the little larva, or triungulin, possesses grasping legs and jaws exquisitely designed for hitching a ride on a pollen-collecting female bee who will inadvertently deposit the triungulin in her nest where it will devour her hard-earned brood provisions.)

The digger bee males zoom about emergence sites, digging for mates that they sometimes uncover. Why this mating system instead of hilltop territoriality *à la* tarantula hawks or scramble competition at a feeding site *à la* blister beetles? Digger bee behavior makes sense if the critical determinant of male mating strategy is the distribution of receptive females. The female bees emerge in substantial numbers in places that their males can easily locate because the males have emerged earlier in the same general location. Freshly emerged tarantula hawks and blister beetles are dispersed across the desert landscape. Therefore the male digger bee, but not the wasp or beetle, can search profitably for emerging females, and indeed male bees may acquire as many as three females in one morning, judging from observations of marked individuals.

But what pressure has favored the evolution of the ability to detect preemergent females? Female digger bees mate just once, storing all the sperm they will need from that single mating. Males who locate many virgin females will propagate their genes more effectively than males who encounter fewer virgins or any number of mated females. Long ago a male who could detect a female just after she emerged or just after she had gnawed an opening to the surface would have been in a better position to leave descendants than males that waited until the virgins had become airborne. The premium on early detection should have favored any male who happened to possess better olfactory sensitivity to virgin females. The reproductive success of these males has meant that males with keen olfactory ability have become very widespread in the population. Currently males are so sensitive that they can find a buried female before she has even completed her exit tunnel.

Male digger bees not only display exceptional skill at sniffing out females, they also wrestle pugnaciously for possession of mates. Latecomers often discover a digging male, having detected the alluring female odor coming from a digging site. Spirited disputes arise over possession of these sites, for the male in charge of the excavation site when a female bursts to the surface has the best chance of inseminating her. Once mated, the female will not accept other sperm that would dilute the first male's fertilization chances. Takeovers of digging sites occur, and even after a pair has begun to copulate, the male may be assaulted by his ungenerous fellows and supplanted before he completes the mating.

The spirit of reproductive competition permeates the lives of male digger bees, affecting the time of emergence (early, to be in line for as many emerging females as possible), the choice of mate-searching area, the sensitivity to certain olfactory cues, and the readiness to engage in violent confrontations over possession of virgins.

Which brings us back to female digger bees and palo verdes. After she acquires a complement of sperm sufficient to fertilize all her eggs, a female leaves her emergence site and soon sets about the construction of a descending tunnel in some appropriately friable soil. At the end of the tunnel she builds an amphora-shaped brood pot set vertically, six to eight inches beneath the soil surface. Once dried, the brood pot becomes a firm, watertight container (nectar, mandibular secretions, and water all may be used in forming the pot — no one knows for certain). Into the amphora the female deposits pollen and nectar, collected generally from palo verdes, although ironwood, which flowers somewhat later, also is an important source, especially in those years when many palo verdes fail to bloom.

A palo verde in full flower would seem to offer an embarrassment of riches for a foraging pollinator, but by now we should be suspicious of the view that individuals will invest heavily in something for which they do not receive a reproductive return.

81

Our suspicion is well-founded, for today's palo verde flowers bear the imprint of reproductive competition among palo verdes in the past. The ultimate goals of a palo verde are, first, to maximize the fertilization of its own flowers with pollen from other trees and thereby maximize production of seeds with its own genes, and, second, to facilitate the transmission of its pollen to other trees of its own species, the better to inject its genes in the seeds of other palo verdes. Both outcomes will improve its chances of leaving descendants. These goals can be advanced if a tree attracts *flower-constant* pollinators that will visit many of its unfertilized flowers and then, covered with its pollen, reliably travel to another palo verde, rather than to a mesquite or ironwood.

The first trick, then, is to communicate with effective pollinators, advertising flowers that have not yet been fertilized and making it worthwhile for pollinators to visit these flowers preferentially. The tree accomplishes this in two ways. It ceases production of costly nectar and pollen in flowers that have been fertilized, and it alters the appearance of these flowers so that bees can identify them as low-profit flowers. For example, the distinctively colored banner petal of the flowers of the blue palo verde folds down over the stigma after fertilization has occurred.

The task of a female digger bee, zipping about in her tasteful desert hues of elegant gray and warm brown, is to maximize the rate at which she collects nectar and pollen. The faster she fills one brood cell, the sooner she can get on with the job of digging a new burrow and forming a new brood cell to fill. The number of surviving offspring she will produce should be increased if she forages as efficiently as possible. Her efficiency is increased if she can quickly find the productive flowers on a tree, and the palo verdes assist her in this.

Foraging gain also increases if a bee is flower-constant. A female digger bee that has learned how to extract pollen and nectar easily from a blue palo verde benefits by going to a series of trees of this species, rather than switching randomly to new flower types, such as ironwood blooms or mesquite catkins, that require somewhat different extraction tactics. Blue palo verdes make it easy for a digger bee to do the efficient thing by having conspicuous, *distinctive* flowers.

There is one seeming exception to this rule. The foothills palo verde and blue palo verde often grow in close proximity. Their flowers appear similar in structure and color to human eyes, but not to bees that can see ultraviolet light, for the ultraviolet reflectance patterns of the two species of palo verde differ dramatically.

C. E. Jones and his colleagues have performed experiments in which they have tied a floral bouquet composed of freshly cut branches of foothills and blue palo verdes onto limbs of selected trees. They then recorded the number of visits by female digger bees to the two introduced species, each of which was represented by about fifty blossoms. The digger bee females mainly visited the flowers in the introduced bouquet that matched those of the tree onto which they were tied. Thus, they foraged nearly exclusively at the added blue palo verde blooms on blue palo verdes and at the experimentally introduced foothills palo verde flowers on trees of this species. Only one visit in twenty represented a switch of species in midstream; digger bees do attend to ultraviolet patterns and use them to be efficiently flower-constant.

The biology of palo verdes and digger bees together constitutes an intricate web of adaptation. Female bees competing with other females race to collect food for their offspring as quickly as possible, taking advantage of the signals the tree provides to encourage full pollination of its flowers. The enormous supply of nectar and pollen produced by dense populations of palo verdes supports large numbers of bees. By often nesting in large groups, mother bees create conditions that favor males who emerge in time to search the emergence site for a series of virgins. Once inseminated, the female bees will carry on the symbiotic relationship with palo verdes that is the legacy of their ancestors.

Ravens

In the warmth of the early morning my shadow stretches between palo verde #10 and its neighbor. The reddish *Bromus* grasses rub shoulders in the wind. A mourning dove flutters down and stands in the dark band of my shadow. A brilliant baby-blue circle of skin rings the dove's tense, uncertain eye. It turns once, then waits, head held high, scanning for danger. Suddenly the dove explodes into flight and dives down the slope on noisy wings, leaving my shadow to shade the dry stones and dying grasses.

Far below two black ravens drift along, tracing the corrugations of the ridge with their inky wings. One bird follows the other; a harsh croak breaks the great silence of the day.

In the forest of thin green stalks of a Mormon tea shrub, a vine has twisted and turned in a race with summer. Six small winged seeds cling to the vine.

At the base of the ridge two young men in search of snakes pry and topple large rocks from places where they have rested for millennia. Black holsters ride their hips. Revolvers at the ready, they stop to ask about rattlers and then, faces wet with sweat, return to their hard work.

Saguaro

A red-tailed hawk curls through the superheated air of noon-time. In three competent revolutions it rises from low on the slope to a point just above the peak. With a shake of its tail, it heads off in a slightly descending glide to the southeast. The hawk's talons enclose a small dark form; a thin tail dangles life-lessly from the bird's claws.

With hardly a flap the hawk covers four hundred yards in a flash, traveling the last hundred feet unusually close to the ground. A swoop of its broad brown wings and it rises abruptly to land on its nest, a great collection of guano-whitened twigs fitted neatly like a Chinese puzzle within the upstretched arms of a massive saguaro. Four chicks, close to fledging, wait panting in columns of shade cast by the limbs of the cactus.

No plant better represents Sonoran habitat than the saguaro cactus. Its distribution practically defines the limits of the desert. A saguaro cannot grow in places where the temperature stays be-low freezing for twenty-four hours in a row, although it can and does tolerate a rare brief snowfall. Its temperature requirements restrict it to the Sonoran region, where the cactus provides much of the distinctive character of the desert. Although not the largest or most massive cacti, an honor held by the Mexican cardon, the saguaro combines large size and aesthetic form extremely well. Its presence relieves the uniformity of a creosote flat or a jumbled forest of palo verde. Saguaros stand only twenty to thirty feet high, but still they rise well above the other vegetation, majestic green statues with pleated bodies that can expand when water can be collected and stored. Each ridge on trunk and limb bears a defensive row of cross-pointed spines that runs the length of the pleat.

The saguaro has always attracted the special interest of visitors and residents of the desert. An Indian name, *sa-war-o*, has given rise to many variants in Spanish or English, some as bizarre as *zuwarrow*. But whatever the spelling, saguaros (the "g" is silent) figured prominently in the reports of early explorers in the area. One of these men, J. R. Bartlett, reported in 1854 that it was not uncommon to see saguaros in the vicinity of what is now Yuma, Arizona, with arrows projecting from them, a form of vandalism magnified a thousand times by current desert dwellers armed with high-powered rifles and shotguns. Apparently there is something about the cactus that invites assault, although the Tohono O'odham people of central Arizona considered it sacrilegious to damage one of these plants.

The Tohono O'odham depended on the fruits of the cactus as a major source of food. Saguaros produce large waxy flowers in May and early June, at a time when the color of the desert is fading fast with the decline of the palo verdes. In a few weeks the flowers will have been pollinated and have given rise to fruits, half the size of a man's fist, which sit in clusters on the tips of the main trunk and arms of mature saguaros. The sweet, nutritious, and brilliantly crimson pulp of the fruits attracts a diversity of consumers, among them curve-billed thrashers, white-winged doves, and the Tohono O'odham, who used to collect fruits with giant poles fashioned from the long, thin, internal ribs of a fallen saguaro. Nonhuman consumers (and perhaps human ones) pass some of the many seeds through their digestive systems unscathed. A seed may be deposited in a favorable spot and the saguaro parent reaps a reward for having induced an animal to consume its sugary fruit.

That saguaros depend on seed-dispersers may help explain an evolutionary puzzle: Why is it advantageous for the plant to grow so tall? The costs to a saguaro of its pattern of growth and reproduction are far from trivial, and saguaro seedlings grow with painful slowness. This is true of cacti as a group: they have waxy surfaces that greatly reduce water loss, but by the same token their structure prevents the rapid exchange of gases and the capture of carbon dioxide, so that their photosynthetic rates are re-markably low. They represent the opposite end of the spectrum from the desert annuals, which have high transpiration rates and correspondingly high photosynthetic activity — and a short life. At ten years of age a saguaro will be only a few inches tall; to reach a height of fifteen feet requires sixty to one hundred years, and fifty years may elapse before a saguaro produces even a single flower. So to grow tall takes a tremendous amount of time and greatly delays the date of first reproduction. By the time many individual cacti can reach flowering age they will have fallen prey to wood-rats or rabbits, or bacterial infection, or accidental death in thun-derstorms. (Only fourteen of eight hundred young transplants survived more than six months in one experiment; almost all were eaten by rodents.)

Even after reaching a respectable height, the saguaro continues to grow, becoming ever more massive and running an ever greater risk of being toppled by a high wind. A mature saguaro weighs many tons, much of it in its upper arms, so that older plants be-come decidedly top-heavy. In one area of wind-thrown cacti I found that the toppled individuals had an average of more than five limbs longer than three feet, whereas the average for a sample of still-standing specimens was two and half large limbs. As one would expect, older, larger saguaros are more likely to be blown down. True, the mechanical features of their internal anatomy are beautifully designed to reduce this risk. The "skeleton" of a sa-guaro consists of a central tube of plant ribs, each about two inches wide. The column of partially independent ribs in the main trunk and arms gives the cactus considerable flexibility, so that it sways with rather than resists the winds that flow about its rounded form. But the system, although mechanically brilliant, is not per-fect. Once overthrown in a violent wind, a saguaro's life and fu-ture reproductive chances come to an irrevocable end.

So why should the plant grow so large and continue growing even after achieving a great height? A question about the life-history tactics of any plant (or animal) is unlikely to have a neat and simple answer, but perhaps part of the reason for the sa-guaro's growth pattern is related to its pollinators and seed distributors. The cactus belongs to a group of plants that relies heavily, but not exclusively, on certain species of bats to pollinate its flowers. These bats tend to employ vision, rather than sonar, to locate sources of food. And the flowers of saguaros offer rich supplies of food — abundant, energy-rich nectar and digestible pollen that provides extraordinary amounts of protein (saguaro pollen contains twice as much protein per unit weight as the pollen of insect-pollinated cacti such as prickly pear or barrel cactus).

Donna Howell notes that many bat-pollinated plants have convergently evolved similar floral characteristics that make it easy for bats to find and remove the rewarding nectar and pollen. First, the flowers themselves are large, conspicuous, and open, enabling a nectar-drinking bat to thrust its whole face easily into the flower. Second, the flowers are located on tall, conspicuous pedestals that could be detected, potentially, at a great distance on moonlit nights.

The "behavior" of bat-pollinated agave century plants provides an instructive comparison with saguaros. Century plants spend many, many years growing slowly, forming more and more massive stiletto-pointed leaves, like a kind of huge blue-gray artichoke. Then, one year, from the center of the "artichoke" springs an enormous asparagus-like stalk, reaching twenty to thirty feet above the leaves whose nutrients have produced it. The stalk sprouts an elaborate candelabrum of highly scented flowers, uncluttered with leaves or other obstacles that might impede night-visiting bats who come with long tongues to drink the nectar. As the bats move between century plant stalks, pollen adheres to their foreheads and fertilizes the flowers that they visit. Once a century plant flowers, fruits, and produces seeds, it dies, a glorious example of the "big bang" reproductive pattern. An individual spends its entire life preparing for a single, all-consuming burst of reproduction, followed by death. Donna Howell suggests that the taller the agave, the more it projects above the desert scrub, the more likely it is to be seen and visited by bat pollinators. If an agave attracts many flower-constant visitors, it should set more seeds and produce more potential offspring. The selective advantage of advertising one's flowers might favor the extraordinary investment in tallness.

The same argument applies with equal force to saguaros and the pollination of their flowers. There may be an added advantage as well for a tall saguaro if the plant gains by attracting certain birds to its fruits. Like the showy flowers, saguaro fruits are conspicuous and easily harvested by animals that can fly to and perch upon the tops of the cacti. Birds probably do an excellent job of dispersing saguaro seeds; white-winged doves and curve-billed thrashers move easily through the desert, and they produce many small fecal deposits. Together these features may increase the chances that one of the saguaro's seeds (and a single cactus can produce two hundred fruits, each with two thousand seeds, and thus four hundred thousand propagules in one year) will miraculously fall to a spot where it can grow. Perhaps tall saguaros attract more superior dispersers than short ones. Rodents and peccaries eat a great many fruits of smaller cacti, and if they could reach the fruits of saguaro they would consume these too. As earth-bound mammals, they have smaller home ranges than white-winged doves and so might fail more often to disperse saguaro seeds as effectively as birds. Broader seed dispersal by birds could favor individual saguaros that placed their fruits high out of reach of wood rats. Moreover, the higher the fruits, the more easily they might be spotted at a distance by doves and thrashers, improving the odds that a saguaro's entire seed crop would be consumed and scattered abroad.

Whatever the reason, we have cause to rejoice in the tallness of the plant. It provides not only visual relief in the desert landscape and food for many insects, birds, and bats, but also safe living space for still more creatures. The larger birds of prey such as redtails, Harris's hawks, and great horned owls nest well above ground among its prickly limbs. Smaller species such as Gila woodpeckers and flickers chisel cavities in the trunks and limbs. After the woodpeckers have moved on, leaving behind a curved, empty cylinder of scar tissue, ash-throated flycatchers and elf owls move into the wonderfully smooth, protected nestholes.

The cactus is then a central element in the ecology and economy of the desert. The Tohono O'odham were right to ostracize anyone who damaged a saguaro. In any case, to shoot a saguaro is fundamentally unfair. A saguaro cannot respond to its assailant but stands pitted and disfigured with wounds that may become infected with fungi or bacteria that will kill the plant. At least once, however, a saguaro has struck back. A few years ago two sportsmen traveled from Phoenix to the desert to exercise their rifles on saguaros. One of the men, David Grundman, tried to blast a limb from a massive cactus with repeated volleys of .72-caliber slugs. He succeeded. The severed arm fell upon him, killing him promptly. His last utterance was at first reported to be the first syllable of "timber," although later the Maricopa County Sheriff's Department concluded that he had called out the name of his companion, Jim; James J. Suchochi was not prosecuted by the state of Arizona for "mutilation of a protected native plant," a misdemeanor for which he could have received a three-thousand-dollar fine and a jail sentence.

Teddy-bear Cholla

A fresh bobcat scat and the clean imprint of a bobcat's paw decorate the trail's edge this morning, clear announcements of an animal that I have never seen, despite many daytime trips to the ridge. The bobcat's signature is a reminder of the great clan of nocturnal creatures that visit the ridge only when the sun has set. For desert animals, nightlife offers the obvious advantages of reduced water and temperature stress; when the stars come out, so do squat black beetles, waxy brown centipedes, and squadrons of scorpions that leave the shelter of their hiding places under the rocks or within abandoned rodent burrows. They wander across the desert floor, sharing a dim world with the occasional bobcat, peccary, or deer, mammals that also make their living in the darkness.

Although many animals can escape the desiccating Sonoran sun by disappearing into daytime retreats, desert plants must stand their ground. Today the teddy-bear cholla seem aflame as May sunlight scatters through the thousands of long creamy-white spines that cover the cactus. From a thin black trunk the limbs radiate out in top-heavy profusion, rather like a Kachina doll with an elaborately spiny headdress. The limbs are segmented, prone to fracture at the constrictions; spiny grenades lie everywhere on the ground beneath the plants.

The essence of this intermediate-sized cactus lies in its thick yet translucent coat of needles, rather than in its flowers, which, unlike those of the saguaro or hedgehog cactus — are small and inconspicuous — a pale greenish yellow that blends into the predominantly buffy hue of the plant. The barbed spines, tapered to an exceptionally fine point, pierce skin and cuticle with the greatest of ease. A tiny fly hangs suspended in midflight, run through by a rapierlike spine into which it had blundered while attempting to land on the cactus. On another cholla, the impaled body of a fledgling thrasher dangles upside down, beak open, eyes closed.

Human visitors quickly make the acquaintance of cholla after their arrival in Arizona. A brush of a forearm, a step taken without care, and there the thing is, a plump whitish sausage of spines caught lightly on an arm or on the side of a shoe, almost as if it jumped to hitch a ride. But it did not have to jump, only barely touch the skin of an unaware person. The spines hurt. No one seems to know what is on the tenacious tips of cholla spines, but whatever it is, it produces the sensation of a bee sting. A flip of the arm meant to dislodge the nuisance only hooks more spines into one's flesh. A reflex grab to remove the now very painful cluster of spines, and a hand fastens grimly to the cactus. After one tar-baby experience with cholla, a person will remember this plant, if no other, and will examine desert trails with respect. An early traveler in Arizona wrote, "The plant is the horror of man and beast. Our mules are as fearful of it as ourselves."

But the spines do more for cholla than educate people, and mules, to desert realities. The fearsome spines are so densely packed that they completely cover the surface of the cactus and protect it from larger insects and mammals that might otherwise consume the plant. Whereas peccaries and rabbits sometimes slice the flesh of young saguaros, prickly pears, and staghorn cactus despite their spines, they are more reluctant to mouth teddy-bear cholla.

In addition to thwarting some herbivores, the thicket of spines may also protect the plant against the sun, scattering and diffusing potent rays, shading the photosynthetic portion of the cholla, cooling it by as much as twenty degrees compared to a portion from which the spines have been experimentally removed.

The barbed spines may also play a small role in the plant's reproductive strategy. Unlike most other desert plants, teddy-bear cholla reproduce primarily by dropping autotomized limb segments to the ground, where they may root and become offspring. If spines hook into a passing mammal, the animal may transport the cholla joint to a new site where it may set down roots. But more often, descendants of cholla spring up close around a parent plant from which they fell, creating over time a dense patch of the cactus, each individual genetically the same as the founder plant from which it budded. The clumped clonal pattern of cholla differs greatly from the much more evenly dispersed distribution of the hedgehogs, saguaros, and other cacti. Unlike teddy-bear cholla, which produce only a few muted flowers, saguaros and hedgehogs invest heavily in the production of large showy flowers, designed to attract animals that will carry pollen back and forth among individuals of their species. Fertilized flowers give rise to fruits with seeds, each of which has its own unique genetic makeup formed through the union of a female sex cell with a foreign male cell carried in a pollen grain.

Why do teddy-bear cholla reproduce largely through asexual budding, creating descendants that are genetic copies of the parent, whereas saguaro and hedgehogs create offspring, each of which is genetically distinct? Evolutionary biologists still debate the reasons for the evolution of sexual reproduction, but some years ago George C. Williams pointed out that asexual propagules of plants tend to be large and develop close to the parent, whereas sexual propagules are small and widely dispersed. Each cholla joint that falls to the ground represents a large investment; cholla do not grow rapidly and the tissues in a joint require years of growth to produce. Moreover, prior to autotomizing a propagule, the cactus covers the joint's surface with a thick coat of excreted wax, the better to conserve the moisture in the limb after it falls to the ground. But the large investment in spines, waxes, and water-laden tissues presumably improves the probability that the potential offspring will actually survive and become established, although Stan Szarek and his students have found that wood rats harvest and eat almost every fallen joint! The joint cannot go far, unless transported by an unfortunate carrier, but this means that it will likely experience soil and microclimate conditions similar to those its parent has exploited successfully. Having the identical genotype as its parent, the offspring may do well too in this portion of the desert.

In contrast, a saguaro, by placing its tiny seeds in an edible fruit, encourages certain animals to disperse its potential progeny hither and yon. They will fall by chance throughout the desert, encountering conditions unlike those faced by the parent plant. Having the same genetic makeup as the parent would be of no special assistance to a dispersed seed propagule and could even be a liability. By creating a huge variety of genetically diverse seeds, the saguaro gambles that a few of its potential offspring will be deposited by chance in places for which their novel genetic constitution happens to be well-suited. When a saguaro reproduces sexually, it plays a lottery with tens of thousands of low-cost tickets (little seeds) that are broadcast widely in the "hope" that one or two might hit the jackpot and survive.

Thus the kind of descendant propagules generated by the asexual cholla and sexual saguaro seem well-suited for the solution of different kinds of problems in development close to and far away from a parent. Sexual reproduction should evolve when an individual can leave more surviving descendants by dispersing its offspring into unpredictably variable environments. Asexual reproduction should spread through populations when the individual can make more surviving copies of its genes by having young that will develop close to it in a more predictable, already tested environment.

But saguaro and teddy-bear cholla often grow close together in the same general area. Do their habitats really differ? Are there more opportunities for asexual reproduction in the places colonized by a cholla than in the nearby locations where saguaros grow? Perhaps the few cholla seeds that are produced are especially adept at settling on and surviving in unusually barren rocky soil in which few other plants can grow. Once a lucky seed becomes established in such a spot, there might be considerable "open" space nearby that the adult plant's cloned offspring can fill. In contrast, saguaros seem to live in somewhat more heavily vegetated portions of the desert. They may gain by disseminating offspring further because there may be little chance that a propagule will encounter a niche open to its development nearby. But we must admit that no one understands enough about the ecological requirements of young cacti and adults of various species to measure the degree of availability of colonizable space about a parent plant. Nevertheless, the differences between chollas and saguaros help us think about these matters and provide a puzzle eminently worth solving.

The cholla, oblivious to the many lessons illustrated by their ferociously spiny limbs, stand prepared for the decades ahead, safe at least from cactus thieves.

Tiger Whiptails

The early morning sunlight irregularly illuminates the west-facing slope of the ridge. It is already eighty degrees and on the way to ninety-five. A fledgling loggerhead shrike pursues its parent across the slope, flying in and out of shafts of sunshine, its black, gray, and white plumage alternately brilliant and subdued. The juvenile alights close to its parent on the long flexible stalk of an ocotillo. The vibrantly red flowers at the tip of each stalk seem mismatched with the wilted, burnt-edged little leaves that line the ocotillo branches. It has not rained in many weeks, and the plant has begun to discard the leaves it produced in green abundance after winter and spring rains. But water conservation does not apply to the flowers, large numbers of which embellish the ocotillo. Soon, however, the tubular flowers will lie on the stony ground, faded images of their once exuberant selves, while small greenish fruits mature on the limbs above them.

The young shrike calls insistently, a whining, demanding note. The parent has no food, and it wings on to a new perch down-slope. A harshly rasping cactus wren inches up the stalk toward the abandoned young shrike; the wren fully extends its wings in threat. The fledgling hesitates and then jumps from its perch, to float downhill after its parent.

Beneath the ocotillo, a tiger whiptail slinks over the desert gravel, pressing its body and long tapered tail close to the ground. The angle of its head changes in herky-jerky movements. With beady eyes the lizard looks ahead and then dashes explosively across an open area, the chocolate-black vertical stripes on its sides blurring as it runs. Once in the shelter of a bursage, the lizard resumes its mechanical movements, then stops, turns its head slightly, and darts forward to snuffle among the debris. A click of its jaws reveals that it has found a sluggish beetle or termite whose body will now contribute to the whiptail's future searches.

A red racer waits with reptilian patience in the shade of a nearby brittlebush for the whiptail to come to it.

Whiptails delight a watcher with their constant activity and bright alertness. When the temperature rises to about eighty degrees, they go on the move, always on the lookout for a meal, a predator, or a rival. Despite awkward-looking, stubby legs that project out at right angles to the long axis of the animal's trunk, a whiptail can fly across a mountain slope, veering from bush to bush, almost leaving a trail of dust hanging in the air behind it.

When two large-headed and black-throated males meet, they usually spring wildly together into a Keystone Kop game of tag, the leader zigging and zagging and the pursuer right on the leader's tail but rarely catching up. Occasionally, however, two males will meet one another belly to belly, arms flailing in a madcap wrestling match that ends as suddenly as it began with the precipitous departure of one of the combatants.

Whereas the hilltopping tarantula hawks and hairstreaks protect perch-scanning sites that may be visited by receptive females in search of male partners, male whiptail lizards defend areas whose food supplies may attract females to the spot. Thus most suitable areas have a resident male and one or more females that live and forage in the area. These animals can be recaptured or resighted day after day during the breeding period from April through July.

Not that mating lizards abound on the ridge. A wary whiptail — and there is no other kind — generally spots intruders before he is spotted and sails to safety rather than pursue a courtship, even under the eye of a sympathetic biologist. Professional herpetologists have seen whiptails mating in the field relatively few times. I have seen it once while showing the ridge to David Crews, a professional herpetologist who wished to noose a few whiptails to take back to his laboratory at the University of Texas. We happened on a male so intent on a mating chase that he did not see us but instead continued to sidle up to the female and, when she moved, to scamper to block her path with his belly. He approached, the female scuttled away, he approached again and again. Finally the female held still as the male slid his chin along her tail and back and gripped her neck in his jaws while curling his body around her trunk. A male lizard has a double penis, one for use if he approaches the female from her right side, the other if he curls about to make contact from her left. Our male inserted the appropriate hemipenis and copulated with his now quiescent mate. Crews, not an extreme romantic, inched forward and grabbed them both with his hand. Into his collecting sack they went.

I did not begrudge Crews the lizards. He had an Arizona permit and the animals were to be transported alive to the comfort of his well-stocked Texas laboratory. He caught a few more, not by hand, but with a noose. The trick in noosing lizards is to inch toward a foraging animal, fishing pole in hand, whereupon one attempts to induce the lizard to place its head through a small loop of monofilament at the end of the pole. Occasionally a lizard will cooperate with this scheme, although much more often either whiptails slip nonchalantly past the noose or else grasses and twigs thwart efforts to place the noose in the proper position. When everything worked as planned, Crews would yank up quickly and a whiptail would fly into the air to dangle for a moment before it was released and dropped into a muslin bag.

Crews wanted Usery Ridge lizards because he studies closely related species of whiptails whose females produce offspring without receiving sperm from males. Thus both asexual and sexual reproduction have evolved in these animals. Unlike a cholla plant, however, which may both flower and drop off limb joints to reproduce, an individual whiptail is completely committed to either an asexual or a sexual mode of reproducing. My lizards belong to a sexual population in which there are males and females.

As with teddy-bear cholla, the puzzle is why sexual reproduction persists in an organism that has the capacity to reproduce asexually. The parthenogenetic female that does not require insemination would seem to have a reproductive advantage compared to a sexual competitor. Let's say that within a sexually reproducing population a parthenogen appears by mutation. Furthermore, imagine that both types are equally efficient at converting food into offspring, so that both will have an average of two surviving progeny. Sex ratios in most sexual species typically are about one to one; females in such species usually have equal numbers of male and female offspring. Therefore, sexual females in our hypothetical population will tend to have one son and one daughter, whereas the asexual parthenogen will produce two female offspring. In a single generation the number of parthenogenetic females will have doubled (from one to two). In the next generation the parthenogens will again produce daughters only and their numbers will double again, whereas the sexual females will merely replace themselves with an equal number of daughters because of the investments diverted to sons. The process, if continued in a stable population, will inexorably result in the eventual replacement of the sexual females by the parthenogenetic types. In areas in which any parthenogenetic females occur, there are usually no sexual types at all.

The question is, What is there about the environment of some whiptail populations that prevents the spread of mutant individuals able to dispense with sex and the need to produce sons? Needless to say, this is a general question that could be asked of any organism, ourselves included, and not just whiptails. The lizards and some asexual fishes show that there is nothing to prevent a vertebrate from practicing parthenogenesis successfully. If the cholla were to be our guide, we might hypothesize that the environment of asexual females should be more stable and predictable than areas in which sexual populations occur. If the daughters of asexual females were guaranteed the same ecological circumstances as those under which their mothers flourished, a parthenogenetic female could reap the advantages of increased production of daughters and have a respectable chance that her genetically identical offspring would survive. In areas with unstable and unpredictable environmental variation, some of the genetically diverse offspring of a sexual female might survive, whereas clones of genetically identical offspring might all perish if they failed to find the exact, limited set of conditions they needed. If so, a sexual female, even though she could produce daughters at only one-half the rate of an asexual rival, could leave more *surviving* descendants than a mutant parthenogen.

To illustrate the degree to which the problem of sexuality is unresolved, let me note that there is a plausible alternative hypothesis that completely dismisses the importance of an unpredictable *physical* environment as the key factor in the evolution of sexual reproduction. Graham Bell has pointed out that if one surveys the biological world as a whole — an exhausting task but one that Bell has managed to accomplish — one finds asexual reproduction strongly associated with disturbed habitats, those that experience great (and unpredictable) fluctuations in physical conditions. For example, among groups of related animals whose representatives occur in both freshwater and marine habitats, asexual reproduction occurs predominantly in freshwater species, sexual reproduction in those that live in the more stable ocean. Freshwater streams and ponds are far more subject to fluctuating conditions than seas and oceans. Moreover, the highest proportion of asexual species are found in small bodies of fresh water, such as intermittent streams or ephemeral rock pools. Bell and others have argued that in stable environments more species can coexist in large numbers, creating a more complex *biological* environment with the possibility of more complex parasite-host, predator-prey interactions. These workers believe that sexuality has evolved under these conditions because sexual individuals are able to produce genetically unique offspring that may be better able to escape their parasites and predators, which have become adapted to genotypes present in the parental population of their hosts or prey.

If this view is correct, we would expect asexual whiptails to be living in association with more frequently disturbed, marginal habitats with fewer parasites and predators than their sexual counterparts elsewhere. Unfortunately, no one has tested this prediction. Thus the puzzle of sexual reproduction persists in whiptails and other species; as a male, I have reason to be thankful that this is so, even if it does pose a continuing problem for evolutionary theoreticians.

100

Horned Lizards and Harvester Ants

A family of cactus wrens drifts across a brown hillside, gliding on mottled wings from one jojoba to another. As they conduct their search, they converse in chuckles, rasps, and soft growls. A wren cocks its head and looks with a piercing eye into the foliage above it. Its scimitar beak reaches up and deftly plucks a pale green katydid from its perch, like a surgeon selecting precisely what he wants from an assistant's tray. After crushing the insect, the wren consumes it with a toss of its head; two hops later it is out of the shrub and on its way to terrorize insects elsewhere.

Only the remnants of spring are left. All is still on the peaktop with the exception of a broken straggle of harvester ants moving toward their nest entrance to escape the fierce sun. There is no wind, only heat radiating from bleached stones. Unexpectedly, a small piece of desert rises from the ground. It scuttles into the partial shade of a shrub whose blackened and leafless limbs cover a portion of the ant nest. From desert colors and desert forms a horned lizard miraculously reconstitutes itself before my eyes. A fringe of thick spines projects backward from its flattened head, like the nape guard of an extinct *Stegosaurus* dinosaur.

With a quick snap of its armor-plated mouth the lizard plucks a harvester ant from its trail. After eating the ant, the lizard remains still and after a while begins to fade as the pattern of the desert gradually absorbs its image.

Horned lizards are probably more common than they appear to be on Usery Ridge. Their carbuncled and flattened bodies blend so beautifully with the hillside that, unless the reptile moves, there is little chance of seeing it. The lizard has a line of hairlike projections from its side that touch the ground when the animal crouches low. These projections eliminate even a trace of shadow by smoothing the union of lizard with its substrate. A horned lizard, hugging desert soil, is usually so confident of its camouflage that it will not stir unless prodded by its disbelieving discoverer.

A comparison of the horned lizard and tiger whiptail demonstrates again how pleasing diversity in nature can be. The whiptail's body pattern, although not ostentatious, is not obviously cryptic, whereas the horned lizard offers a classic case of camouflaged coloration. The whiptail relies heavily on vigilance and speed to outrace its enemies; the horned lizard is a slow and clumsy runner who puts all its money on not being visible to its predators. Whiptails also have a long and fragile tail, with fracture planes built into some of the tail vertebrae for ease of breakage should a predator grasp the appendage. In populations of the lizard, anywhere from one-quarter to three-quarters of the adults will have lost a tail at least once. The removal of a tail is a serious matter for a whiptail because it contains some of the animal's fat reserves. It will cost the lizard considerable energy to regenerate a new one, but better to lose some energy than to lose life itself. Horned lizards have little stubby tails not readily autotomized. The chance that a predator would capture them by the tail is very low, whereas a sparrow hawk or leopard lizard might often grasp the tail of a rapidly darting whiptail.

Differences in the speed of the two animals correlate with their distinctive foraging patterns — the whiptail zipping from shrub to shrub in search of termites and other small insects, the horned lizard stationing itself by an ant nest where it can wait for ants to transport themselves to their doom.

The ability of horned toads to eat harvester ants arouses awe in those of us who have handled the ants. These thick-bodied, big-jawed ants possess a potent stinger that conveys a deeply painful toxin to those unfortunate enough to annoy them. For a human, pain endures for twenty-four hours or longer. Yet horned lizards consume harvester ants almost to the exclusion of all else. Harvester ants make up over 90 percent of the diet of these predators, thanks in part to their great tolerance to ant toxin.

Given its ability to ignore ant stings, one would think that, once a horned lizard had found an ant colony, it would polish off huge numbers of workers in one mammoth meal before moving on to the next colony. But in real life a lizard daintily snaps up a few workers here and there on the fringes of foraging trails and the edge of the nest apron and then departs, leaving behind multitudes of uneaten prey. One possible explanation of this puzzle is that the lizard is a "prudent predator" that does not deplete a colony so severely that it cannot return to it productively at a later date. When the worker force of a harvester ant colony falls sharply, the ants may close up shop and remain underground for a time before venturing forth again. The prudent-predator hypothesis suggests that a lizard with a "trapline" of colonies that it visits repeatedly, each time removing a small number of victims per colony, is a lizard who over the long haul gains more calories and nutrients than one that drives the workers underground so that they cannot be harvested for many days.

There is, however, a problem with the prudent-predator hypothesis: in the interim between visits to a colony by a prudent lizard, the ants conserved for later harvest might instead be eaten by a transient lizard, whose reproductive interests are best served by maximizing its immediate gain without regard for the long-term productivity of an ant colony. Only if a horned lizard had an exclusive foraging territory would it gain from prudent predation. Otherwise what one lizard left for its future, other lizards might well consume for their own benefit.

Do horned lizards have feeding territories? Patrolling the area in which a number of ant nests were located would be difficult for a horned lizard, given its greatly limited mobility. There is no evidence that individuals are able to maintain an exclusive feeding preserve. Thus the prudent-predator hypothesis is unlikely to be correct.

Instead, Steven Rissing has suggested that horned lizards appear to exercise restraint in attacking ants, not because of any long term foraging considerations, but because of the short-term consequences of arousing a colony of ants. Every time a worker is crushed in the powerful jaws of a horned lizard, alarm scents spew from the deceased ant, scents that may lead other ants to approach and attack the cause of alarm. Many species of ants do mob horned lizards aggressively; this is effective not so much as a method of stinging the lizard into retreat, given the lizard's immunity to stings, but because the mob of ants draws attention to the lizard and makes it vulnerable to animals that prey on it. In effect, the ants could strip the predator of its camouflage, exposing it to roadrunners and shrikes, hawks and coyotes. This makes it advantageous for a lizard to feed unobtrusively and avoid the risk of detection by workers that could give the signal to mob.

In this context, the prey preferences of horned lizards begin to make sense. The desert horned lizard feeds overwhelmingly on a species of harvester ants that forages as solitary individuals. These ants rarely join forces to attack the lizard en masse, whereas group-foraging species that travel in large numbers can do this and are much less likely to be chosen by the lizard. In fact, one harvester species that lacks a sting altogether rarely attracts horned lizards. It is the most social of foragers and the most aggressive in swarming over a lizard when one is discovered near a food-gathering column.

Horned lizards and their prey appear to be engaged in a long evolutionary struggle: the lizard now is able to tolerate potent stings, but attacked ants sometimes respond by mobbing the predator into retreat. The battle between predator and prey doubtless will continue, with selection favoring those variants on either side that are better able to overcome the opponent's stratagems.

In the meantime, a horned lizard waddles slowly across the barren desert floor and flings itself onto a dark rock that has been warmed by the early morning sun. The lizard sprawls, body draped over the rock, looking like an exhausted swimmer collapsed upon a beach.

Wood Rats

A large rattler lies across the trail at palo verde #10, stopping me in my tracks. Syrphid flies hover calmly in the lee of the tree above the immobile snake. The gray rattler, with glazed eyes and lumpish body, fails to rattle and refuses to move even when I toss a few pebbles in its direction. When I return a short time later, the snake has drifted off to rest somewhere out of view.

A wood rat, a favorite prey of rattlers, has piled a great mound of desert debris on the steep hillside beneath palo verde #10. The rodent lives within a den covered with palo verde twigs, the skeletons of staghorn cacti limbs, and, amazingly, the spiny joints of teddy-bear cholla. The den's occupant suddenly scampers from its home and runs along a little trail that it has lined with pieces of cholla and other cacti remnants. The diamondback has not captured this rat yet. Suddenly the wood rat stops, looks at me (perhaps with dismay), and dashes back to the safety of its nest. Its large eyes, useful in nocturnal rambles, appealing round ears, and soft gray body are swallowed by the mouth of its den.

An orange-crowned warbler dives into the palo verde above the wood rat's nest, its greenish yellow feathers merging with the delicate greens of the tree. One of the last tarantula hawks of the spring cruises slowly past on damaged wings, still intent on combat, but a diminished image of its once powerful self.

Wood rats have earned a measure of fame, or notoriety, thanks to their relentless search for objects to add to their dens. These animals are known commonly as pack rats or trade rats, the latter name reflecting the sentimental, but incorrect, belief that wood rats leave behind a gift for each item taken, trading a cow chip for a watch or a ring, a stick for a set of false teeth. The inadvertent donors of watches and false teeth must have concluded that wood rats strike a hard bargain.

The energetic pursuit of den-building by wood rats produces impressive results. C. T. Vorhies and W. P. Taylor estimate that an average den contains about twenty cubic feet of material scavenged from the desert, item by item. In heavily grazed areas, the animal does the best it can with cow-chips, but in other locations wood rats make their homes where chollas thrive most densely, using joints of the cactus to cover their living places. The devastating spines of teddy-bear cholla do not deter white-throated wood rats. Instead with careful incisors they grip a fallen joint by its sparsely spined internodal area and pull the cholla sausage gingerly backward toward the den to line a foraging trail or to go on top of the heap. A wood rat can even snip off a patch of spines without becoming impaled to get at the tissues of the cholla. After devouring the edible portions, the rat will place the cholla husk with its remnant spines on the den. The moisture in cholla and other cacti help the wood rat meet its water needs so that it never drinks water directly.

Wood rats are not alone in making use of the protection offered by cholla cactus. A number of desert birds, notably the cactus wren but also curve-billed thrashers and mourning doves, regularly nest within a prickly tangle of cholla limbs. Although some snakes can somehow cautiously slither up and into cholla-guarded nests, most predators wisely refuse to poke around amid spines so potent and numerous.

The use of cholla joints has its risks for desert wood rats and birds alike because of the accidents that can occur; young animals in particular may become entangled in the very material that was to have been their protection. Baby wood rats sometimes die, hopelessly stuck to the cholla on the dens of their mothers.

Nor can cholla repel all the enemies of wood rats. One of those unfazed by the cactus is a cuterebrid bot fly, a massive black insect with unwholesome gray blotches on its abdomen. Female bots lay their eggs at the dens of wood rats. The minute larvae, after hatching, wait for a chance to enter the body of the resident wood rat through the rodent's nose, mouth, anus, or vagina. Most bots wait in vain and perish. But a few seize an opportunity and, by climbing aboard, they invade their host to travel eventually to a site just under its skin. There they feast on wood rat tissues and grow into huge engorged grubs, forming tumor-like bulges in the body of a victim. An unlucky wood rat may have as many as four or five larval grubs living within it, but in most places bots are rare, happily for the local rats.

Only when it is ready to pupate does the bot larva leave the wood rat, burrowing through its host's skin to pop out into the litter of the den where it pupates. The wood rat, relieved of its parasite, generally survives the experience. The bot pupa gives rise to an adult in due course. After several days of maturation, the fly is ready to begin the reproductive phase of its life. Like tarantula hawks and great purple hairstreaks, adult female bots are scarce and widely distributed throughout the desert, in part because wood-rat dens are scattered widely. Bots do not feed as adults and live only ten to fifteen days on the reserves obtained from their rodent victims. Thus a male has only a short time in which to locate females. Males that tried to find mates by waiting at a den or by visiting a series of wood-rat nests would have little chance of success because of the very low probability that a recently emerged female would be available for mating at any one den. In any case, females mate just once some days *after* emerging. Not surprisingly, therefore, wood-rat bots are hilltopping insects. In the absence of any more profitable strategy, males fly to Usery Ridge and other mountains in the area. There they perch on the ground in open areas along the backbone of a ridge to wait for the rare passing female. As she buzzes past, a male will chase and capture her; the pair tumbles to the bursage on the slope below the peak to mate, after which the female begins her hunt for the dens of wood rats while her partner returns to his perch site.

Although females visit the ridge infrequently, a male's wait is far from uneventful. Just as is true for the wasp and hairstreak, male bots compete furiously for favorite perching places — but only during a two-hour period in the morning. As the season progresses, the territorial time shifts earlier and earlier, beginning at 9:00 or 9:30 A.M. in February and ending by 8:30 or 9:00 A.M.

in late May, as the bots avoid both chilly and exceptionally hot temperatures. During the daily flight period, bots arrive at a number of places along the ridge, most often at the highest point where they alight on pebbles and stones on the barren upper portion of the peak. There may be just one male or three, four, even six individuals, perched plumply at scattered points about the site. Whenever two or more bots use the peak simultaneously, they will interact with one another sooner or later. Typically as an incoming bot drones toward a landing spot, a perched male will fly up to meet him. Bots employ several flight speeds, but when they chase one another they stay exclusively in high gear. Despite their chunkiness, flying bots are all but invisible to an observer, such is their rapidity of movement. An early estimate of bot-fly velocity had the insects traveling in excess of six hundred miles per hour, a wonderful figure but rather too generous because a fly traveling at this speed would require more than its own weight in metabolic fuel for each second of flight. Bots just *seem* to be flying hundreds of miles per hour.

Even though they are hard to see in aerial combat, bots are easy to follow. Particularly on still mornings they sound like diminutive race cars, zipping noisily first this way and then that as they charge back and forth over the ridge and peak. A pursuit lasts no more than three minutes; usually just one fly returns to perch on the peaktop.

In order to make sense of the chaos of zooming flies, I did what I had done to the tarantula hawks and hairstreaks. I captured bots in an insect net, a feat that required a certain amount of stealth and a violently rapid downward swing of the net over a perched male. (Bots cannot be taken after they become airborne.) Once each male was marked with dots of Liquid Paper or enamel paint, sometimes fancifully applied as racing stripes on the thorax, I released him. With delightful equanimity, most returned within a few minutes to the peaktop and entered the fray again with vigor.

Marking individuals helped enormously to clarify the social structure of males at the peak. On the majority of days, one male arrived early, fought often, and stayed late in the morning, while some other flies, usually a total of five or six, but sometimes as

many as eighteen, visited the site for much shorter intervals, occasionally for thirty to forty-five minutes, more often for a minute
or two (just long enough to engage the resident male in one
chase). Visitors invariably left after having zoomed about the area
with the resident. Thus it appears that one male "owned" the
peaktop perching area and repelled intruders with high-speed
chases. These flights, like those of the wasps and butterflies, never
resulted in grappling or wrestling. They seemed designed to test
the flight speed and maneuverability of an opponent, perhaps to
demonstrate to slower, less agile males that they would be unlikely to outrace the faster bot to a passing virgin female.

A successful territory defender was almost certain to return
again first thing the next morning, and he might succeed in defending his perching-scanning spot another day. But it was the exceptional fly that remained at the peaktop three full mornings in a
row. Eventually a resident male became an ex-resident when he
abandoned the area to another male, generally after a long series
of spirited chases. Ex-residents sometimes returned briefly to visit
their old territory, but in a few days they would be dead, their
adult lives having raced away from them. The bodies of fallen
bots, perfectly preserved in the dry heat of the desert, remained
on the ridge, their wings tattered, their enormous but lifeless eyes
staring blankly at the sky overhead.

June

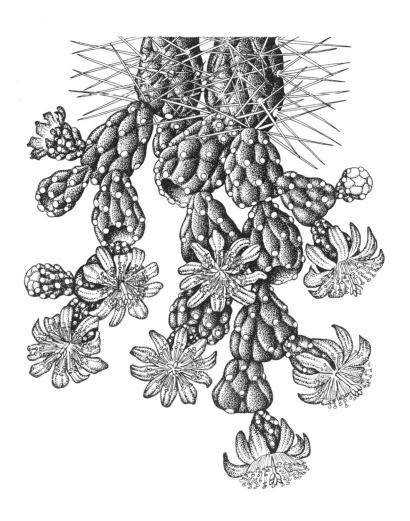

Illustration: Chain-fruit cholla

Summer

W ave after wave of heat breaks over the ridge, even though it is still early morning. One last bot fly, a true survivor, perches on the lonely peaktop. Its frayed wings bear the imprint of battles with competing males that are no longer alive. The sky above the peaktop palo verde contains no spiraling tarantula hawks, nor is there the buzz of even one digger bee on the ridge. The palo verdes are barren. The harvester ants refuse to venture out in the scorching heat; they have gathered sufficient quantities of seed to last them through the summer.

No quail or raven calls from the ridge. No gunfire comes from the gravel pit. The desert is quiet except for the wind. A fractured desert-tortoise shell rests in the wash below. The brown scutes of the shell have partly fallen away to reveal a smooth, white skull-like skeleton; the disarticulated bones of one leg lie a few feet away.

The seep has been reduced to a trickle, hardly more than a damp spot in the sand. A mourning dove clatters out of a mesquite and wings off down the wash, passing over a nearly upright beer can, half-buried in fine gravel.

But the ironwoods glow with pale magenta blossoms and the chain-fruit (or jumping) cholla will soon join them, for their buds are close to bursting. These are the last of the major desert plants to flower. The chain-fruit, like its cousin the teddy-bear cholla, produces a few small flowers, delicate and lovely but inconspicuous blossoms that project from the dangling fruits of previous years. (The fruits of the chain-fruit cholla evidently are not meant for eating but instead are retained by the plant. From last year's fruits come this year's reddish blossoms, which in turn give rise to a new link in the chain. Eventually, portions of chain-fruits may fall and perhaps give rise vegetatively to descendants.)

Ironwood could hardly be more different in its pattern of flowering. In years when the proper conditions apply, these trees, like palo verdes, metamorphose from a rather ordinary green shrubby plant to a glorious burst of color produced by thousands of flowers. The exact nature of the color changes with every shift of viewing angle and every alteration in the position of the sun. A luminescent purple, a subdued pink, a flat blue-gray — all are possible in the chameleon-like tree. Female digger bees forage urgently at the flowers, as if they know that the ironwood flowers are their last, brief chance to harvest. Soon the desert floor beneath the ironwoods will be obscured by the ghostly gray fragments of myriad flowers, fragments that will dry and disappear. But the trees will survive. They and the other natural inhabitants of the desert have the evolved capacity to deal with the predictable onslaught of summer, which, unlike the novel and inventive assaults of civilization, can be endured.

I hike back up the wash, crunching grit and pebbles beneath my feet. In some sections brown grasses obscure the lines of fine gravel deposited when water last ran here many months ago. A clean footprint appears unexpectedly in the sand, sending a surge of adrenaline and fear quickly through me; who else could be here today? But it is my own footprint that shortens my breath and steals the pleasure of desert solitude.

Alone, I push on through layer after layer of resisting heat. My canteen rests lightly, nearly empty, in my pack. From a spiny cholla perch, a panting cactus wren stares at me and then reluctantly spreads its mottled wings to sail away, taking life with it past the still palo verdes and jojobas. A silence remains behind that envelopes the desert world as tightly as the woven heat.

A New Spring

Illustration: Gila woodpecker nest in giant saguaro

Giant Saguaro

The desert has prepared itself for a new spring. The terrible relentless days of summer that dragged on into October finally yielded to fall and winter. On the ridge the palo verdes and brittlebush responded to late-summer thunderstorms and winter rains by producing fresh leaves in abundance; the desert is once again counterintuitively green.

But apart from seasonal alterations, little else has changed. The pattern of the desert persists from one year to the next. Black-throated sparrows twitter from staghorn cacti. The shrubs and trees and cacti stand much as they did the past spring.

There is one special exception. The giant saguaro collapsed and fell during a violent August windstorm.

An observer can count hundreds of saguaros in the plain below Usery Ridge. Many of these magnificent cacti have three or four or five huge arms, upstretched from thick trunks, reaching fifteen to twenty-five feet into the air. They may be 150 or even 200 years old. But in previous springs one saguaro, thirty-five feet high with a trunk nine feet in circumference, towered above all the others. Its massive trunk, almost black with age in its lower sections, supported a small army of limbs, thirty in all, that rose vertically like giant organ pipes. This cactus must have weighed at least twice as much as any other saguaro for miles around, and there could not have been many more impressive individuals anywhere in the Sonoran desert.

If it had been merely big, this giant saguaro would have been a curiosity, nothing more. But there was a special symmetry to the ancient cactus. It was huge but graceful in its affirmation of life. No person had pocked its flesh with bullets, perhaps because no one could fail to admire, even revere, this saguaro, but perhaps also because it was a half-mile from the nearest track and therefore not easily reached by the local gunners.

How old was this saguaro — 250 or 350 years? I have the feeling that there are several common size classes of saguaros in the Usery area. Perhaps all the members of one size class were established in the same decade or the same year when some exceptional combination of circumstances made it possible for the plants to survive long enough to escape the appetites of herbivores. Such a year or decade might come along once every century or so. Was the saguaro giant the last representative of its age class, a group that once predominated 200 or 300 years ago but was reduced by age, accident, and disease to this one plant? The saguaro presided over the desert like a question mark.

Last spring in a hole in one limb, Gila woodpeckers had a nest from which echoed the faint yammerings of hungry nestlings. The adults hurried back and forth in the undulating flight of woodpeckers, carrying food to their offspring. When a parent landed by the hole, insect in beak, the young birds within began to scream insistently until the adult woodpecker entered, distributed food, and left, empty-beaked.

A great mass of twigs perched clumsily on the tops of several neighboring limbs, like an ill-fitting toupee. On my visits I often heard the strangulated call of the builder of the nest, a Harris's hawk perched on its observation post on a nearby, much smaller saguaro. The hawk had streaked the limbs of the giant saguaro with its white guano.

I discovered the death of the giant saguaro in the late summer when, after an absence of several months, I went back to the ridge to reacquaint myself with the desert. Taking the trail to the peaktop, I then descended to the major wash below before cutting across the gullied plain on the west of the ridge. Memory directed me toward the spot where the giant saguaro grew, a mile or so distant. At first my failure to see the massive arms above the palo verdes and ironwoods puzzled me. But with dismay I soon realized that I had not forgotten where the giant grew, for it lay on the desert floor before me. Its massive trunk had fractured and splintered near its base. The largely intact body of the saguaro reached cleanly across the ground, although a few limb tips and arms lay scattered about where they had been thrown by the tremendous force of the saguaro's collision with the desert. As it toppled, the cactus carried with it branches of the ironwood tree that grew nearby. The majestic permanence of the saguaro had been a mere illusion, and its death left me with a disturbing sense of betrayal.

Today, a half-year later, the giant saguaro remains remarkably complete. It and the many other saguaros that fell during the storm still lie mostly green and whole, their bodies pointing to the south. Here and there the pale ribs of a limb peek through a crack in the drying cuticle of the cactus. Desert fruit flies drink in clusters at brown fluids oozing in slow decay down the pleated trunk, while orange syrphid flies hover noisily among the deflated limbs.

The day fades like other spring days as the evening robs the desert of its color. The distant silhouettes of still-standing saguaros have lost the crisp greenness of morning. They rise darkly against the sky, slightly askew, like Indian totems abandoned by men for centuries.

Appendix

Scientific names of some frequently mentioned species

African daisy	*Arctotis* sp.
Barrel cactus	*Ferocactus wislizenii*
Blue palo verde	*Cercidium floridum*
Brittlebush	*Encelia farinosa*
Bursage	*Ambrosia deltoidea*
Century plant	*Agave parryi*
Chain-fruit cholla	*Opuntia fulgida*
Creosote bush	*Larrea tridentata*
Fiddleneck	*Amsinckia* sp.
Foothills palo verde	*Cercidium microphyllum*
Hedgehog cactus	*Echinocereus engelmannii*
Ironwood	*Olnyea tesota*
Jojoba	*Simmondsia chinensis*
Lupine	*Lupinus* sp.
Mesquite	*Prosopis juliflora*
Mistletoe	*Phoradendron californicum*
Ocotillo	*Fouquieria splendens*
Poppy	*Eschscholtzia mexicana*
Prickly pear cactus	*Opuntia* sp.
Saguaro	*Carnegiea gigantea*
Staghorn cholla	*Opuntia versicolor*
Teddy-bear cholla	*Opuntia bigelovii*

ANIMALS

Ash-throated flycatcher	*Myiarchus cinerascens*
Black-tailed gnatcatcher	*Polioptila melanura*
Black-tailed jackrabbit	*Lepus californicus*
Black-throated sparrow	*Amphispiza bilineata*
Bot fly	*Cuterebra austeni*
Bruchid beetles	*Mimosestes amicus* and *Stator limbatus*
Cactus wren	*Campylorhynchus brunneicapillus*
Collared peccary	*Tayassu tajacu*
Coyote	*Canis latrans*
Desert tortoise	*Gopherus agassizi*
Diamondback rattlesnake	*Crotalus atrox*
Digger bee	*Centris pallida*
Gambel's quail	*Callipepla gambelii*
Gila woodpecker	*Centurus uropygialis*
Great purple hairstreak	*Atlides halesus*
Harris's hawk	*Parabuteo unicinctus*
Harvester ant	*Pogonomyrmex* sp.
Honeybee	*Apis mellifera*
Horned lizard	*Phrynosoma platyrhinos*
Meloid ["blister"] beetles	*Lytta magister* and *Tegrodera aloga*
Mourning dove	*Zenaida macroura*
Phainopepla	*Phainopepla nitens*
Raven	*Corvus cryptoleucus*
Red-tailed hawk	*Buteo jamaicensis*
Robin	*Turdus migratorius*
Spadefoot toad	*Scaphiopus* sp.
Tarantula hawk	*Hemipepsis ustulata*
Tiger whiptail lizard	*Cnemidophorus tigris*
White-throated swift	*Aeronautes saxatalis*
White-throated wood rat	*Neotoma albigula*
White-winged dove	*Zenaida asiatica*

Selected Bibliography

The Sonoran Desert

Crosswhite, F.S. and C.D. Crosswhite. 1982. *The Sonoran Desert.* In *Reference handbook of the deserts of North America,* ed. G. Bender. Westport, Conn: Greenwood Press.

Usery Ridge

Marcus, L.N. 1983. The spatial and temporal evolution of the Tonto National Forest. Unpublished master's thesis, Arizona State University.

FEBRUARY

Three Robins

Anderson, B.W., and R.D. Ohmart, 1978. Phainopepla utilization of honey mesquite forests in the Colorado River valley. *Condor* 80: 334–38.

Cowles, R.B. 1972. Mesquite and mistletoe. *Pacific Discovery* 25: 19–26.

Cowles, R.B., and E. S. Bakker. 1977. *Desert journal.* Berkeley: University of California Press.

Walsberg, G.E. 1977. Ecology and energetics of contrasting social systems in *Phainopelpa nitens* (Aves: Ptilogonatidae). *University of California Publications in Zoology* 108: 1–63.

White-throated Swifts

Beecher, M.D., and I.M. Beecher. 1979. Sociobiology of bank swallows: Reproductive strategy of the male. *Science* 205: 1282–85.

Lack, D. 1956. *Swifts in a tower.* London: Methuen.

The Great Purple Hairstreak

Alcock, J. 1983. Hilltopping territoriality by males of the great purple hairstreak, *Atlides halesus* (Lepidoptera: Lycaenidae): Convergent evolution with a pompilid wasp. *Behavioral Ecology and Sociobiology* 13: 57–62.

Robbins, R.K. 1981. The "false head" hypothesis: predation and wing pattern variation of lycaenid butterflies. *American Naturalist* 118: 770–75.

Tarantula Hawks

Alcock, J. 1981. Lek territoriality in a tarantula hawk wasp *Hemipepsis ustulata* (Hymenoptera: Pompilidae). *Behavioral Ecology and Sociobiology* 8: 309–17.

———. 1983. Consistency in the relative attractiveness of a set of landmark territorial sites to two generations of male tarantula hawks (Hymenoptera: Pompilidae). *Animal Behavior* 31: 74–80.

Thornhill, R., and J. Alcock. 1983. *The evolution of insect mating systems*. Cambridge: Harvard University Press.

Diamondbacks

Smith, R.L. 1982. *Venomous animals of Arizona*. University of Arizona, Tucson: Cooperative Extension Service.

APRIL

Desert Annuals

Schaffer, W.M., D.W. Zeh, S. L. Buchmann, S. Kleinhaus, M.V. Schaffer, and J. Antrim. 1983. Competition for nectar between introduced honeybees and native North American bees and ants. *Ecology* 64: 564–77.

Brittlebush

Carrel, J.E., and T. Eisner. 1974. Cantharidin: Potent feeding deterrent to insects. *Science* 183: 755–57.

Ehrlinger, J., O. Björkman, and H.A. Mooney. 1976. Leaf pubescence: Effects on absorptance and photosynthesis in a desert shrub. *Science* 192: 376–77.

Smith, W.K., and P.S. Nobel. 1977. Influences of seasonal changes in leaf morphology on water-use efficiency for three desert broadleaf shrubs. *Ecology* 58: 1033–43.

———. 1978. Influence of irradiation, soil water potential, and leaf temperature on leaf morphology of a desert broadleaf, *Encelia farinosa* Gray (Compositae). *American Journal of Botany* 65: 429–32.

Desert Tortoise

Hohman, J.P., R.D. Ohmart, and J. Schwartzmann. 1980. An annotated bibliography of the desert tortoise *(Gopherus agassizi)*. *Desert Tortoise Council Special Publication* 1: 1–121.

Hedgehog Cacti

Gordon, B.B. 1980. Cactus rustling. *Science* 80 (July/August) 1: 52–59.

Varmint Hunters and Other Gunners

Brattstrom, B.H., and M.C. Bondello. 1983. Effects of off-road vehicle noise on desert vertebrates. In *Environmental effects of off-road vehicles,* ed. R.H. Webb and H.G. Wilshire. New York: Springer-Verlag.

Collared Peccaries

Byers, J.A., and M. Bekoff. 1981. Social, spacing and cooperative behavior of the collared peccary, *Tayassu tajacu. Journal of Mammology* 60: 767–85.

MAY

Gambel's Quail

Leopold, A.S. 1977. *The California quail.* Berkeley: University of California Press.

Palo Verde

Gori, D. 1983. Post-pollination phenomena and adaptive floral changes. In *Handbook of experimental pollination biology,* ed. C.E. Jones and R.J. Little. New York: Van Nostrand Reinhold.

Jones, C.E. 1978. Pollinator constancy as a prepollination isolating mechanism between sympatric species of *Cercidium. Evolution* 32: 189–98.

Mitchell, R. 1977. Bruchid beetles and seed packaging by palo verde. *Ecology* 58: 644–51.

Shreve, F. 1911. Establishment and behavior of the palo verde. *Plant World* 14: 289–96.

Shreve, F., and I.C. Wiggins. 1964. *Vegetation and flora of the Sonoran Desert.* Stanford: Stanford University Press.

Digger Bees

Alcock, J. 1980. Natural selection and the mating systems of solitary bees. *American Scientist* 68: 146–53.

Alcock, J., C.E. Jones, and S.L. Buchmann. 1976. Location before emergence of the female bee, *Centris pallida,* by its male (Hymenoptera: Anthophoridae). *Journal of Zoology* 179: 189–99.

Saguaro

Benson, L.D. 1982. *The cacti of the United States and Canada.* Stanford: Stanford University Press.

Howell, D.J. 1976. Plant-loving bats, bat-loving plants. *Natural History* 85 (Feb.): 52–59.

Mitich, L.W. 1972. The saguaro — a history. *Cactus and Succulents Journal* 44: 118–29.

Teddy-bear Cholla

Benson, L.D. 1982. *The cacti of the United States and Canada.* Stanford: Standford University Press.

Hadley, N.F. 1972. Desert species and adaptation. *American Scientist* 60: 338–47.

Holthe, P.A., and S. Szarek. 1985. Physiological potential for survival of propagules of crassulacean acid metabolism species. *Plant Physiology* 79: 219–24.

Williams, G.C. 1975. *Sex and evolution.* Princeton: Princeton University Press.

Tiger Whiptails

Congdon, J.D., L.J. Vitt, and N.F. Hadley. 1978. Parental investment and comparative reproductive energetics in bisexual and unisexual lizards, genus *Cnemidophorus. American Naturalist* 112: 509–21.

Parker, W.S. 1972. Ecological study of the western whiptail lizard, *Cnemidophorus tigris gracilis,* in Arizona. *Herpetologica* 28: 360–69.

Pianka, E.R. 1970. Comparative autecology of the lizard *Cnemidophorus tigris* in different parts of its geographic range. *Ecology* 51: 703–20.

Horned Lizards and Harvester Ants

Rissing, S.W. 1981. Prey preferences in the desert horned lizard: Influence of prey foraging method and aggressive behavior. *Ecology* 62: 1031–40.

Wood Rats

Alcock, J., and J.E. Schaefer. 1983. Hilltop territoriality in a Sonoran desert bot fly (Diptera: Cuterebridae). *Animal Behaviour* 31: 518–25.

Vorhies, C.T., and W.P. Taylor. 1940. Life history and ecology of the white-throated wood rat, *Neotoma albigula albigula* Hartley, in relation to grazing in Arizona. *University of Arizona Agricultural Experimental Station Technical Bulletin* 86: 455–529.

Index

insects, 29; of white-throated swift, 15–16; of wood rat, 106
Nitrogen-fixing plants, 73

Off-road vehicles, 72, 78
Ohmart, R., 54
Olfaction: of digger bee, 79; of meloid beetle, 48

Palo verde, 73–77, 78, 81–83
Parental behavior: of digger bee, 81; of tarantula hawk wasp, 28–29; of peccaries, 63–64
Parthenogenesis, 98–100
Peccaries, 61–68
Pollination: and flower constancy, 82–83; of agave century plants, 88; of annual plants, 43; of palo verdes, 82–83; of saguaro cactus, 89
Poppy, 40
Predatory behavior: of birds, 47; of horned lizard, 101, 102–103; of tarantula hawk wasp, 29
Prudent-predator hypothesis, 103

Rainfall: amount of, 2; as cue for animal reproduction, 70–72; as cue for plant reproduction, 44, 73, 103; needed for seed germination, 43
Rattlesnake: behavior, 33–36; bite, 35
Resource-defence strategy, 31, 48
Rissing, S., 103
Robbins, R., 22

Saguaro cactus: diseases of, 90; growth rate of, 87; life-history

tactics of, 87, 88; mortality of, 87, 117–19; photosynthetic rate of, 87; pollen production of, 88
Salt River Project, 4–6
Schaffer, W., 41
Search image, 47
Seeds: mistletoe, 12, 14; palo verde, 75; saguaro, 86, 89
Sexual competition: in digger bees, 81; in hairstreak butterflies, 24–25; in swifts, 16; in tarantula hawk wasps, 29–30; in tiger whiptails, 97
Sexual reproduction, 93–94, 98–100
Shreve, F., 75, 77
Spermatheca, 50
Spiral flights: of hairstreak butterflies, 24–25; of tarantula hawk wasps, 29–30
Stator limbatus, 76
Sting: of harvester ant, 102; of tarantula hawk wasp, 28–29
Suchochi, J. J., 90
Survival rate: of palo verdes, 75, 77, 110; of saguaro, 175–77; 87, 117–18; of tortoise, 53–54
Symbioses: phainopepla-mistletoe, 13, 14; plant-pollinator, 42, 78, 81–82; plant-seed disperser, 86
Szarek, S., 93

Tail autotomy, 102
Taylor, W. P., 106
Territorial behavior: of bot fly, 107–9; of great purple hairstreak, 22–24; of tarantula hawk wasp, 27, 30

133

About the Author

JOHN ALCOCK received his Ph.D. in biology from Harvard University and is now professor of zoology at Arizona State University. He is the author of *The Masked Bobwhite Rides Again* (1993), *Sonoran Desert Summer* (1990), and *The Kookaburras' Song: Exploring Animal Behavior in Australia* (1988), all published by the University of Arizona Press.